EDUCATION DIVIDES

Poverty and schooling in the 1990s

By Teresa Smith and Michael Noble
with Jane Barlow, Elaine Sharland and George Smith

CPAG Ltd, 1-5 Bath Street, London EC1V 9PY

CPAG promotes action for the relief, directly or indirectly, of poverty among children and families with children. We work to ensure that those on low incomes get their full entitlements to welfare benefits. In our campaigning and information work we seek to improve benefits and policies for low-income families, in order to eradicate the injustice of poverty. If you are not already supporting us, please consider making a donation, or ask for details of our membership schemes and publications.

Poverty Publication 90

Published by CPAG Ltd, 1–5 Bath Street, London EC1V 9PY

Tel: 0171 253 3406

ISBN 0 946744 76 9

The views expressed in this book are the authors' and do not necessarily express those of CPAG.

A CIP record for this book is available from the British Library

Cover and layout design by Devious Designs, 0742 755634
Typeset by Nancy White, 0171 607 4510
Printed by The Alden Press, 0865 249071

CONTENTS

ABOUT THE AUTHORS

Teresa Smith is a lecturer in the Department of Applied Social Studies and Social Research at the University of Oxford, where she teaches community work and pre-school policy. Her main research interests are in the fields of pre-school and family policy, community and poverty, and she has just completed a study of family centres for the Department of Health and the Children's Society which will be published by HMSO in 1995. Recent publications include 'Children and young people – disadvantage, community and the Children Act 1989' in P Henderson (ed), *Children and Communities* (Pluto Press, 1994). She was an elected member of Oxfordshire County Council from 1985 to 1993 and is currently a co-opted member of the Education Committee.

Michael Noble is a lecturer in the Department of Applied Social Studies and Social Research at Oxford University. Before that he was a social welfare lawyer working for a community work/welfare rights project. His major research interests are in the areas of income maintenance policy and poverty and exclusion. Recent publications include 'After redundancy' in T Hayter and D Harvey, *The Factory and the City* (Mansell, 1993, with Ann Schofield) and 'Changing Patterns of Income and Wealth in Oxford and Oldham' (University of Oxford, 1994, with George Smith, Teresa Smith and others).

Jane Barlow, **Elaine Sharland** and **George Smith** are members of the research team in the Department of Applied Social Studies and Social Research.

ACKNOWLEDGEMENTS

We would like to thank the local authorities, schools and parents who contributed to our surveys, and Kath Munby who carried out the interviews with parents; David Bull, Peter Golding, Cyn Mackay, Carey Oppenheim and Joan Sallis who commented on our drafts, and particularly Renée Harris who steered through the final publication; and the many organisations and individuals who provided us with information and helpful leads.

Thanks, too, to Jules Feiffer for giving us permission to reproduce his cartoon on page 28.

FOREWORD

The goal of 'equal access to a first class education' is surely unexceptionable. Yet, as the authors of this report argue in their introductory reflections and demonstrate in chapter after chapter, the reality has been 'a growing educational divide'.

The continuing existence of a *divided* Britain is an obvious matter of concern to the Child Poverty Action Group, especially when the divide is growing.

CPAG's interest in divisive institutions, and in the exclusion of low-income families these entail, stretches across the various services and provisions of the 'welfare state'.[1] But action against child poverty does not require CPAG to comment and campaign, with equal vigour, across all the social services. Any pressure group's priorities are likely to be determined not only by its own resources of time and expertise but by the strength of other groups in a given area of social policy and by changes in the political agenda set by government.

Education has been richly endowed with groups more than capable of promoting the cause of equal access. But, as the early editions of *Poverty* bear witness, CPAG has long been involved in the debate about the relationship between deprived home environments and educational opportunities.[2] The Group's principal focus, though, soon became the vitiation of 'free' education in schools.

Our interest in the right to participate without 'cost' – whether financial or psychological – in free schooling has, of course, informed CPAG's campaigning not just on 'education' but on two other fronts: the 'cost of a child'; and the exclusion imposed by poverty. Indeed, a recent CPAG publication demonstrates, in a way that marries those two themes of childrearing costs and social exclusion, the impact of schools' demands on parents.[3]

Since we reviewed the nature of those demands in 1983/84, after one Thatcher term,[4] there has been a bombardment of education statutes which have broadened the questions of how equal access to our schools can be obtained; of how the consequent obligations of attendance can be fulfilled; and of how fairer and more 'efficient' outcomes can be achieved.

Of course, some of this legislation has effected what the authors describe as 'strictly educational' changes. But the proof of their analysis is the way in which they show that what might initially appear to be 'education-only' issues can often be of crucial concern to the 'poverty lobby'.

At the end of that first Thatcher term, we had suffered only the Education Act of 1980 – 'a small step', it then appeared, but 'the precursor', it was to prove, to 'the much more fundamental reforms' of subsequent Thatcher administrations, to say nothing of the lengthy Act of 1993. That Act was, of course, foreshadowed in a White Paper – *Choice and Diversity* – to which the authors make several references. In dismissing as 'weasel words' the Government's claims for the benefits of 'choice' and 'diversity', one Labour education pundit has suggested how a Labour Government might translate these concepts into a more egalitarian policy.[5]

That vision need not detain us here. For the moment, this book shows how, far from achieving the White Paper claims (see Chapter 1) to equalise opportunities, the reforms of 1980-93 have had a divisive effect. The ideologues have striven to shift the emphasis (see Chapter 3) from a collective responsibility to modify – or at least compensate for – a disadvantageous environment to one of *individual* responsibility.

Early signs of such a shift were recorded in CPAG's first-term audit. Mr Carlisle, as Secretary of State for Education, had declared it 'a natural reaction for parents to provide the best they can for their children'.[6] Our retort was that a responsible government would aim to harness such parental ambition, while redressing the inequalities of opportunity that must follow from its unbridled pursuit. The message of this book is that no such balance has been attempted: on the contrary, the emphasis on individualism has been such as to 'turn attention away from the link between social inequality and educational performance' (see Chapter 3).

This shift has seen 'free' education – to which CPAG had long found much of the education establishment indifferent – joined, on the pyre of unprotected causes, by some of education's more sacred cows. The Thatcherite visions and vocabulary that had become the 'new common sense of social policy' by 1983[7] were reaching out, by 1988, from soft, first-term targets elsewhere in the public sector to areas of education that would have been 'unimaginable' targets in 1979.[8]

After the 1993 Act, then, it was timely for CPAG to review the state of those shifting targets. So it was exciting to learn that not only was pertinent research being conducted in the Department of Applied Social Studies and Social Research at the University of Oxford but that the researchers were ready and willing to report, for CPAG, on their findings of an 'education divide'.

I repeat: to divide has been to exclude. No amount of 'weasel words' can cover up the damage to those children excluded from the opportunity to participate in a free, first-class education.

David Bull
Executive Committee, CPAG

NOTES

1. See, thus, CPAG's report on the impact of the first two Thatcher terms: Alan Walker and Carol Walker (eds), *The Growing Divide: a social audit 1979-1987*, Poverty Publication No. 72, 1987.
2. I have documented the development of that concern in my introduction to a special 'Poverty Focus' on CPAG's interests in education: 'Education: burdening the family', *Poverty*, No. 58, August 1984.
3. Sue Middleton *et al*, *Family Fortunes*, Poverty Publication No. 89, 1994, Chapter 5.
4. See note 2 above and the education chapters in CPAG's report on the first Thatcher term: David Bull and Paul Wilding (eds), *Thatcherism and the Poor*, Poverty Pamphlet No. 59, 1983, Chapters 8-10.
5. Christopher Price, 'School daze', *New Statesman and Society*, 6 January 1995, p24.
6. As cited in that first term review (note 4 above), p57.
7. Peter Golding, 'Rethinking common sense about social policy', in Bull and Wilding (note 4 above), Chapter 2, p7.
8. See Michael Flude and Merril Hammer (eds), Introduction, *The Education Reform Act 1988: its origins and implications*, Falmer, 1990, pix; and Roger Dale, *The State and Education Policy*, Open University Press, 1989, p115.

1

Educational policy and poverty

I am not prepared to see children in some parts of this country having to settle for a second-class education.

John Major, foreword to *Choice and Diversity: A New Framework for Schools*, July 1992

John Major's challenge, set out in the White Paper, *Choice and Diversity,* which preceded the 1993 Education Act, is a powerful one. Do all children have equal access to a first-class education? Or is there a growing educational divide that mirrors the increasing social and economic divisions within our society? That is the central question for this study.

Education and social divisions?

In the last decade, the living standards of the poor and affluent marched in opposite directions ... Poverty means going short materially, socially and emotionally. It means spending less on food, on heating and on clothing than someone on an average income. But it is not what is spent that matters, but what isn't. Poverty means staying at home, often being bored, not seeing friends, not going to the cinema, not going out for a drink and not being able to take the children out for a trip or a treat or a holiday ... Above all, poverty takes away the tools to create the building blocks for the future – your 'life chances'. It steals away the opportunity to have a life unmarked by sickness, a decent education, a secure home and a long retirement.

Carey Oppenheim, *Poverty: The Facts*, CPAG, 1993

INCOME GROWTH AND INCOME INEQUALITY – THE GROWING SOCIAL DIVIDE

Surveys such as that by the Institute for Fiscal Studies (IFS),[1] which analysed the Government's annual Family Expenditure Survey, have shown that despite an overall growth in income in real terms over the last 30 years, the gains have been very unequally distributed. In 1961 the bottom tenth of households had just over 4 per cent of total income while the top tenth had 22 per cent. During the late 1960s and the 1970s, the share of income of the bottom tenth increased to around 4.5 per cent while the share of the top tenth remained the same. Since 1977 there has been a widening gap between the top tenth and the bottom tenth of households. By 1991 the income share of the top tenth had increased to around 25 per cent, while the share of the bottom tenth had fallen to 3 per cent. Looking at the poorest groups, income levels for the lowest 5 per cent, after taking housing costs into account, had fallen from around £73 per week in 1979 to around £61 per week in 1991.

Data from the IFS survey and the Government's own series, *Households Below Average Income* (HBAI),[2] show that in addition to these sharp changes in the shape of income distribution, the *composition* of low-income families demonstrated another important trend. It is particularly *families with children* that have increased as a proportion of those in the poorest groups. Pensioners, a group traditionally concentrated in the lower income bands, have tended to move out of the poorest category as more of them receive occupational pensions. Figure 1.1 from the IFS study (opposite) shows the changing proportions of the bottom 10 per cent of households by family type over this 30-year period, particularly the worsening position of both one and two parent families.

These trends are in line with the latest Department of Social Security figures on income support[3] which show that in 1993 approximately one in four of all dependent children live in households on income support, in Great Britain as a whole, a rise from just over one in five children in 1991. These children are concentrated among the younger age groups – 36 per cent (1.12 million) being under five years, and about the same proportion (1.14 million) of primary school age. The latest HBAI report for 1991/92, which reveals that 30 per cent of dependent children were living in households without a full-time worker (up from 18 per cent when the HBAI series began in 1979), notes with calculated understatement that this change 'gives the family a higher than average risk of being on a low income'.[4] The number of children entitled to free school meals – since 1988 effectively a proxy for income support – has risen in England from 821,400 in 1991 to 1,141,300 in 1993, a rise of nearly 40 per cent.

These figures show both the high overall levels and rapid increase in social and economic disadvantage experienced by many families with children over the last 15 years. Recent studies further reveal that poor families are increasingly concentrated in particular areas. Based on a comparison between the 1981 and 1991 Censuses, Anne Green demonstrates how the degree, extent and intensity of poverty increased in inner London and other large metropolitan areas over the decade; she draws attention to the concentration of poor families in inner and east London and their isolation 'from the social and economic

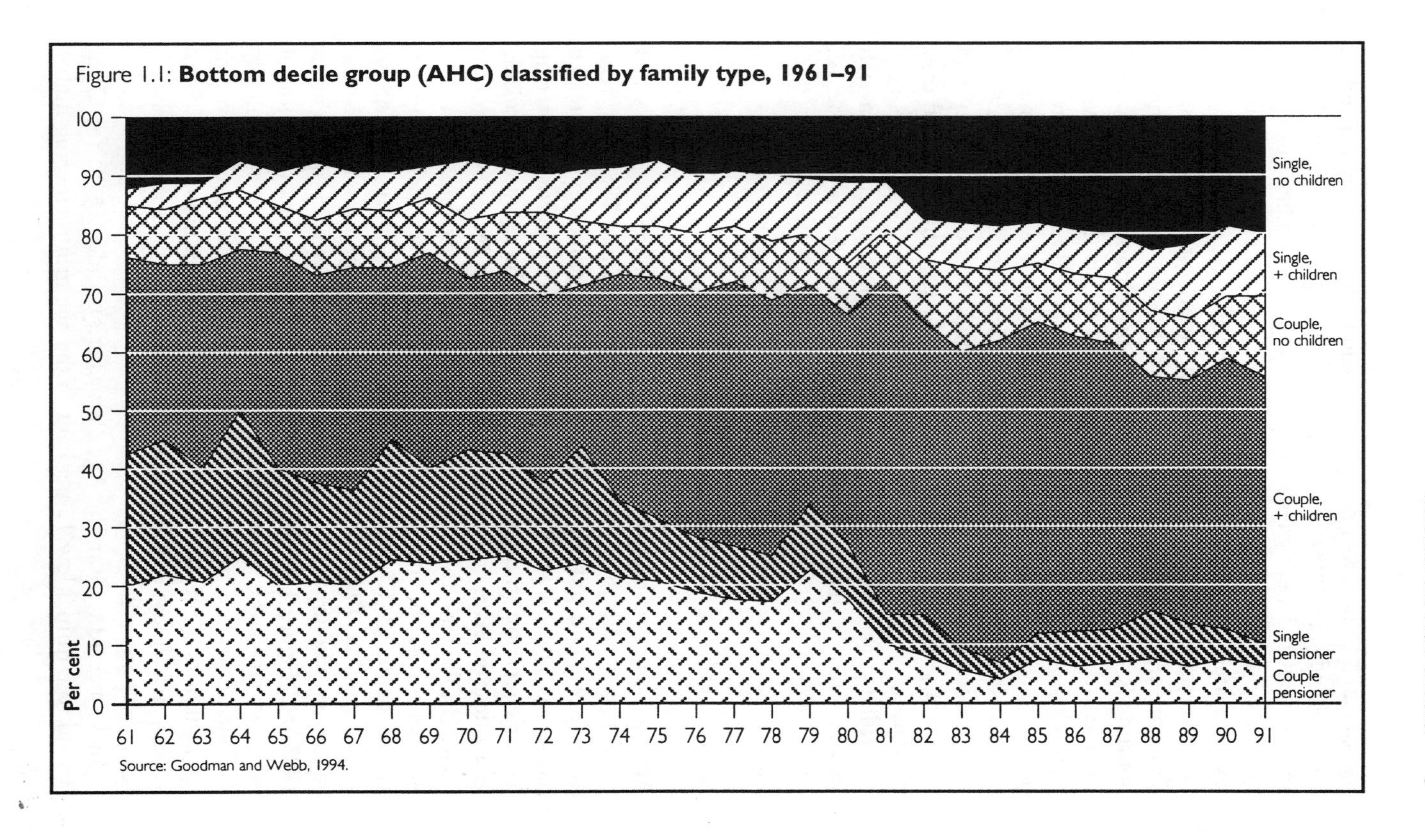

Figure 1.1: **Bottom decile group (AHC) classified by family type, 1961–91**

Source: Goodman and Webb, 1994.

mainstream'. Other areas doing badly include those heavily dependent on single industries now in decline – coal mining, heavy manufacturing and port-related industries.[5] More detailed local studies,[6] using data for the same period, show how low-income families are increasingly concentrated in particular neighbourhoods, especially the more disadvantaged council estates, even in more prosperous districts. Comparisons between 1981 and 1991 suggest that many neighbourhoods with the highest concentrations of poor families in 1981 were actually *worse off in absolute terms* in 1991, with higher levels of unemployment, lower economic activity rates and increasing proportions dependent on means-tested benefits. Meanwhile, better-off neighbourhoods moved sharply in the other direction, with increases in owner occupation, two car ownership, high economic activity and continuing low levels of unemployment. The gap thus widened over the decade.

Evidence for a widening social and economic gulf between rich and poor families is overwhelming. But what has been the impact on education?

AN EDUCATIONAL DIVIDE?

After a period of relative stagnation throughout the late 1970s and early 1980s, education in Britain as a whole since 1988 has been marked by rapid growth in many areas – in qualifications, increased staying-on rates beyond the age of 16 and the proportions entering higher education (though as we shall see later the resources available for education have not risen in line with these increases). Thus, in England following the introduction of the GCSE examination in the summer of 1988, the proportion of school leavers achieving 5+ higher grade (A-C) passes rose from 26 per cent in 1987/88 to 41 per cent in 1993. The proportion of 16 year olds in full-time education rose from 38 per cent in 1979/80 to 73 per cent in 1993/94.[7] Figure 1.2 (opposite) shows the pattern of participation in full-time education since 1983. The change since 1988 is initially attributable to the introduction of the GCSE and to employment opportunities – or the lack of them – for minimum age school leavers, and almost certainly not to the spate of education legislation from 1988 onwards.

In higher education, the Age Participation Index (API) for Great Britain rose from a low 13 per cent of the age group entering higher

Figure 1.2: **Participation in full-time education of 16,17 and 18 year olds 1983/84 to 1993/94**

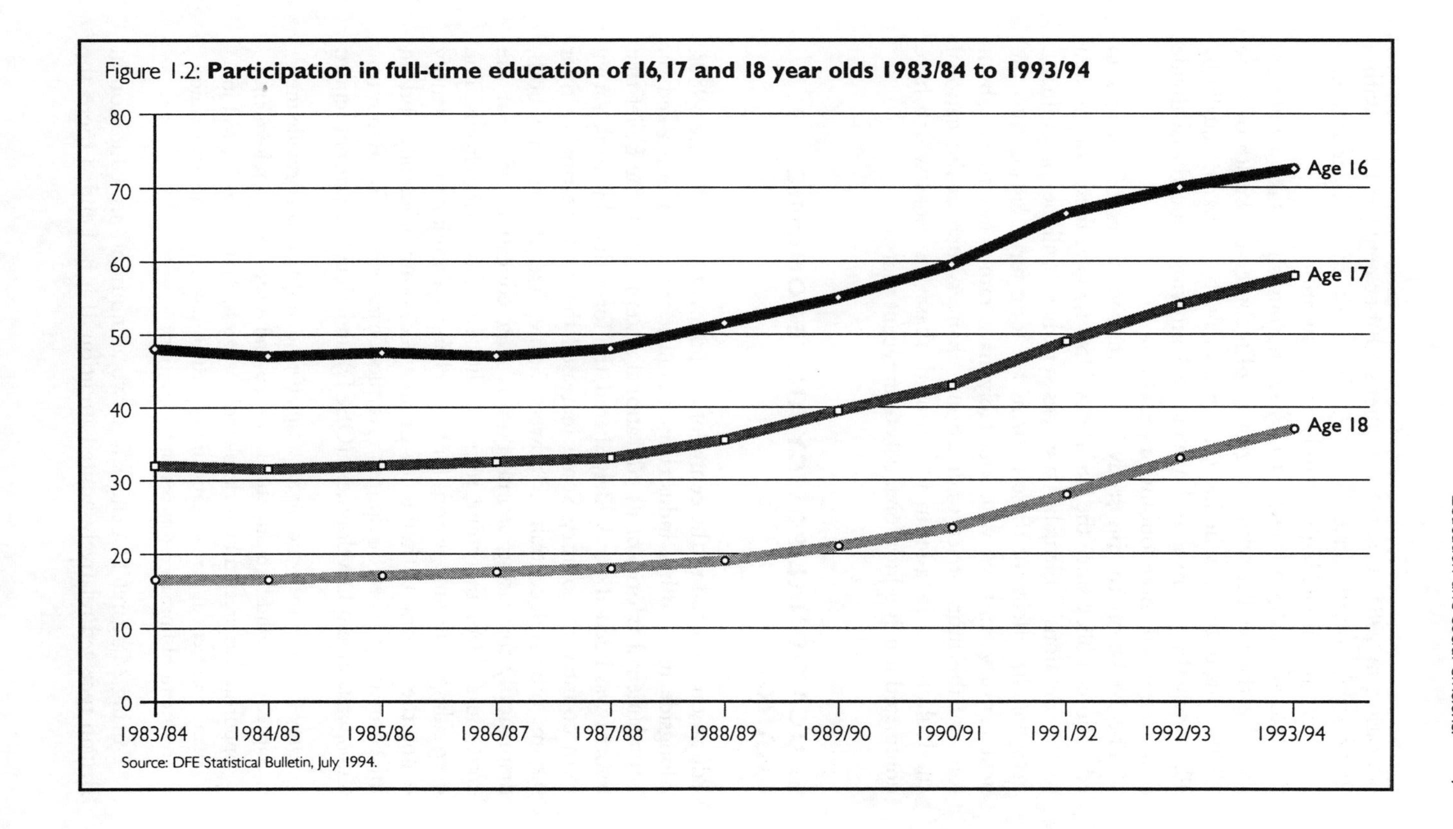

Source: DFE Statistical Bulletin, July 1994.

education in 1981 to a much higher 27.8 per cent by 1992, with a 26 per cent growth since 1990.[8] At first sight, this is clear evidence both for growth *and* higher standards in education.

Amid all this good news, it may seem churlish to take a different line. But the parallel with the growth of income and wealth over the 1980s leads us to ask whether these gains have been shared equally by all, or whether there is still a wide and growing educational divide reflecting social and economic divisions.

The backdrop to this study is the massive series of changes in educational policy since the late 1980s. How far have these contributed to the divisions? Inevitably any answers here will be preliminary: many of the effects of these reforms are long term, lasting into the next century. And we will, inevitably, have rather less to say about some of the more strictly educational changes, such as the national curriculum and its assessment, although these are issues which have dominated much educational debate in recent years.

EDUCATIONAL POLICY AND ECONOMIC CHANGE

Education returned to the centre of the policy stage in the late 1980s. Alongside many other industrialised countries, Britain embarked on a fundamental reform of its educational system. While the belief that reform was needed was widely shared, the form that this took varied from country to country. Some increased the centralisation of their system; others decentralised powers. Some, like Britain, did both, dramatically increasing central powers over education, while at the same time devolving some responsibility to individual schools. The over-riding economic reasons for these changes are not hard to identify – nor the common themes of greater economic efficiency and an injection of 'market disciplines'. As the Organisation for Economic Co-operation and Development (OECD) underlined in a recent report:

> Only a well-trained and highly adaptable labour force can provide the capacity to adjust to structural change and seize new employment opportunities created by technological progress. Achieving this will in many cases entail a re-examination, perhaps radical, of the economic treatment of human resources and education.[9]

During Margaret Thatcher's first two administrations, education in Britain received relatively limited attention. If it had ended there, the

1980 Education Act with its move to increase parental choice might have been seen as a small step. With hindsight, it can be seen as the precursor of the much more fundamental reforms which followed later in the decade. But in the early 1980s the emphasis was elsewhere – not least in programmes for the massive increase in the numbers of unemployed young people leaving school. The Government's explicit aim was to reduce, rather than expand, government expenditure and involvement. It was without irony that a book on educational policy written during this period could be titled *Education – The Wasted Years*.[10] The charge levied against both the Conservative administration and its Labour predecessor was one of neglect and inaction in the field of education.

The 1987 general election, in which education played a prominent part, changed all that, though the first signs of a much more interventionist stance had come with the announcement of City Technology Colleges (CTCs) in 1986. The principal reasons for this shift were clearly stated: a concern that the educational system was *not* responding to changing economic needs and worse, that schools and local authorities might have their own very different agenda; and a fear, fuelled by a series of international comparisons,[11] that educational standards were falling further behind competitor nations.

Since 1988 the school system in England and Wales has experienced an unprecedented series of changes with four major educational Acts, supplemented by extensive sets of regulations, themselves subject to repeated amendment. This has taken education down a legislative road very familiar to those in the social security field. The intention behind these changes was summarised at the start of the 1992 White Paper, *Choice and Diversity*:[12]

> Our reforms rest on common-sense principles – more parental choice; rigorous testing and external inspection of standards in schools; transfer of responsibility to individual schools and their governors; and, above all, an insistence that every pupil everywhere has the same opportunities through a good common grounding in key subjects.

Simply stated, but the result has been a welter of legislation, shelf-loads of circulars and the creation of new Government agencies, set up only to be reformed under the next bout of legislation. The Dearing reviews[13] of the national curriculum and its assessment provided a temporary if welcome relief, before the next wave of change stemming from the 1993 Act, certainly the longest in history, began to come into force.

STANDARDS AND CHOICE

'Standards' and 'choice' with 'accountability' are the watchwords of this market-oriented view of education. The general argument about greater competition and autonomy for schools, and the shift away from 'producer-' or 'supply-' to 'consumer-' or 'demand-led' services, is familiar.[14] The then Department of Education and Science set the scene in the circular accompanying the 1988 Education Reform Act:[15]

> The Government's principal aims for schools are to improve standards of achievement for all pupils across the curriculum, to widen the choice available for parents for the education of their children and to enable schools to respond effectively to what parents and the community require of them, thus securing the best possible return for the substantial investment of resources.
>
> Department of Education and Science, *Local management of schools*, Circular 7/88

In the area of 'choice' there are obvious examples of schools 'smartening up their image', preparing glossy brochures and reverting to school uniform. But the crucial questions are how choice affects schools' educational performance and the distribution of educational opportunities. More alarming, there is evidence from a number of countries which have followed a similar route that greater choice through 'open enrolment' can *increase* social segregation.[16] Some parents will be more active and successful than others in choosing popular schools, and popular schools may well be located in more prosperous rather than disadvantaged neighbourhoods. Schools may become *more* rather than less polarised in terms of their reputation and social class (and ethnic) intake. If this is the case, these policies will *reduce* rather than increase opportunities for children from poor families, by concentrating socially disadvantaged children in a limited number of increasingly unpopular schools. The theoretical choice available to parents is more than matched by the power of the successful school to choose its intake.

STRUCTURE OF THE REVIEW

This review focuses on the effect of these changes on children from low-income families and disadvantaged areas.[17] This is not a new field for CPAG.[18] But the effects for low-income families are no longer confined to questions of free school meals, subsidies for clothing, or indeed the hidden costs of schooling. They are to be seen in the fabric of the education system – in the provision of education itself – and the educational outcomes for different groups of children.

Inevitably we have had to restrict the scope of our study, concentrating principally on the school level, despite the number of changes that have directly affected students during this period (for instance, the introduction of student loans, and students' loss of entitlement to benefits such as housing benefit and income support). But we have included some evidence on the experience of young people leaving school at the minimum age and changes that occurred earlier in the 1980s, including other legislation which has had a direct impact on education.

- First, we focus on the question of **resources and provision**. Do children in particular areas or from particular groups receive different levels of provision or resources? We take this up in more detail in Chapter 4.
- Second, we focus on **access** to different forms of provision – for example, nursery education. Chapters 5 and 6 ask whether policies intended to give more choice to parents in their children's education match the realities of new developments such as grant-maintained schools, admissions policies, and access to pre-school or post-school provision.
- Third, we focus on the **costs of education** to families and of equipping children for school – the costs of meals, school clothing, school trips – and their impact on families on low incomes, as well as the sharp differences in practice from one area to another. Chapters 7 and 8 focus on the costs of schooling for poor families and ask whether education is indeed still a free service.
- Finally, we focus on differences which may prove to be most important in the long run, the **results and outcomes of education** – the extent to which different groups have different levels of success in obtaining qualifications and persisting to higher and more selective levels. We look at the question of performance in Chapter 9.

There are striking differences and anomalies wherever we look, for example, some evidence suggests that expenditure levels on education became *more* varied at LEA level during the 1980s.[19] But the key question is the extent to which these differences are structured, rather than random. This line of enquiry leads to a closer look at the policy background in Chapter 2, and the links between education and social inequality, which are examined in Chapter 3.

NOTES

1. A Goodman and S Webb, *For Richer, for Poorer: the changing distribution of income in the United Kingdom, 1961-91*, The Institute for Fiscal Studies, 1994.
2. Department of Social Security (DSS): *Households Below Average Income, 1979-1991/92*, HMSO, 1994.
3. DSS, *Annual Statistical Enquiry*, HMSO, 1994.
4. DSS, *Households Below Average Income*, p53.
5. A Green, *The Geography of Poverty and Wealth*, Institute of Employment Research, 1994.
6. M Noble, G Smith *et al*, *Changing Patterns of Income and Wealth in Oxford and Oldham*, Department of Applied Social Studies and Social Research, University of Oxford, 1994.
7. Department for Education (DFE), *DFE Statistical Bulletin 14/92*, July 1992; *DFE Statistical Bulletin 10/94*, July 1994.
8. DFE, *DFE Statistical Bulletin 13/94*, August 1994. 'Age Participation Index' is a measure of the proportion of the age group entering higher education. It expresses HE entrants under the age of 21 as a per cent of half the total population aged 18 and 19 years. Figures for Great Britain.
9. Organisation for Economic Co-operation and Development (OECD)/ Centre for Educational Research and Innovation, *Education at a Glance: OECD indicators*, OECD, 1993, p9.
10. M Morris and S Griggs, *Education – The Wasted Years? 1973-1986*, Falmer, 1988.
11. S Prais, 'Educating for productivity: comparisons of Japanese and English schooling and vocational preparation', *Compare*, 16, 1986, pp121-47; S Prais and K Wagner, 'Schooling standards in England and Germany: some summary comparisons bearing on economic performance', *NIESR Economic Review*, 112, 1985, pp53-76.
12. DFE, *Choice and Diversity: a new framework for schools*, Cm 2021, HMSO, 1992, piii.
13. Sir Ron Dearing, Chairman of the School Curriculum and Assessment Authority (SCAA), was asked to review the national curriculum in 1993. His final report, recommending radical slimming down of content, was published in November 1994.
14. For example, M Friedman, *Capitalism and Freedom*, University of Chicago Press, 1965; C B Cox and R Boyson (eds), *The Fight for Education: Black Paper 1975*, Dent, 1975; Hillgate Group, *Whose Schools? A radical manifesto*, Claridge Press, 1986; M Chubb and T Moe, *Politics, Markets and America's*

Schools, Brookings Institution, 1990.
15. Department of Education and Science (DES), *The Education Reform Act: local management of schools*, Circular 7/88, DES, 1988.
16. D Hirsch, *School: a matter of choice*, Centre for Educational Research and Development, Organisation for Economic Co-operation and Development (OECD), 1994.
17. Although some Scottish material is included, this research focuses on England and Wales.
18. See D Bull, *What Price 'Free' Education?*, CPAG, 1980; D Bull and C Glendinning, 'Access to "free" education: erosion by statute and stealth'; C Glendinning with P Dixon, 'School meals: privatisation, stigma and local "autonomy"'; D Bull, '"Free" education: shirking and shifting responsibilities', in D Bull and P Wilding (eds), *Thatcherism and the Poor*, CPAG, 1983.
19. H Glennester and W Low, 'Education and the welfare state: does it add up?', in J Hills (ed), *The State of Welfare*, Oxford University Press, 1990.

2 Educational policy: the social dimension

Since its inception, state education in Britain has been concerned with goals other than simply the 'three Rs'. The introduction of compulsory education from 1870[1] was explicitly aimed at poorer groups. As Forster argued in his speech introducing the Bill, 'only two-fifths of the children of the working classes between the ages of six and ten years are on the registers of the government schools, and only one-third of those between the ages of ten and twelve'.[2] On Forster's reckoning, this left at least 1.5 million children predominantly from poorer areas 'unhelped' by schools. Increasingly such help, often administered via the school attendance officer, tended not to be restricted to education in the narrow sense. Subsidised 'penny dinners' operated in many poorer urban areas in the 1880s, the school health service developed using school explicitly as a route for improving child and family health and other special services began towards the end of the 19th and in the early years of the 20th century.[3] And the provision of free, universal education may in itself be seen as a welfare measure. Yet any suggestion since the mid-1980s that education has a 'social dimension' has been rejected as 'social engineering'.

We can conveniently divide this social dimension to educational policy and provision into four different, but overlapping, stages.

TOWARDS A MINIMAL STANDARD

> It is curious ... to find how prevalent is the belief that immediately after ... the Education Act of 1870 ... every child in England and Wales trooped gladly into school. In reality ... this happy state of affairs was not reached for twenty five years, although in certain

areas something was done to get children into temporary school accommodation.

G A N Lowndes, *The Silent Social Revolution*, OUP, 1969, p21

Compulsory schooling drew attention to a range of social problems affecting young children and provided a point of contact for services to begin the process of improving these conditions, at least to a minimum standard. Thus, the school medical inspection, first recorded in the 1890s, was one of the main mechanisms for identifying the appalling extent of ill-health and related problems among young children. For every 1,000 children in a poor urban area at the turn of the century, there were 'from 150 to 180 suffering from diseases of the nose and throat, from 100 to 130 showing definite signs of malnutrition ... and from 100 to 200 ... with vision so seriously defective as to require the immediate provision of spectacles'.[4]

Faced with these conditions, it is not difficult to see the reason for the emphasis on health services provided through the school and education system and on nutritional standards seen in the spread of school meals provision. The aim of these reforms was to place children on an equal footing in terms of their capacity to benefit from education. Local authorities were empowered to provide meals for children unable 'by reason of lack of food to take full advantage of the education provided for them'.[5]

Other services included school clothing grants and the range of special and welfare services gradually developed over the present century. Attendance officers, established by the 1870 and 1876 Acts, increasingly played a welfare function, often providing food, fuel and clothing to poor families.[6] The intention was hardly to produce equality, but rather to establish minimal acceptable conditions, initially by regulation and then by some form of direct provision of services. The style was distinctly paternalist and 'top down'. The school was a way of reaching through to family and community in the absence of more direct provision.

This theme of welfare and 'minimal standards' has continued to be of importance throughout the 20th century. The 1944 Education Act acknowledged that school attendance officers had both legal enforcement and welfare functions and the professional associations at the time recognised this emphasis by changing their title to 'education welfare officers'.[7] Proposals throughout the 1960s and 1970s for the education welfare service (EWS) continued to accept the dual role of enforcing school attendance and developing broader social work support, with responsibility for these areas oscillating between the new social work departments and the old education departments.[8] The 1980s, however, tipped the balance sharply towards school attendance. A report from Her Majesty's Inspectors (HMI) on the EWS, published in 1984,[9] and the subsequent circular on school attendance and education welfare services, published in 1986,[10] both emphasised the welfare of children, but within an enforcement context:

> The EWS is a service that gets its *raison d'etre* from the obligations and duties placed on parents and LEAs by the Education Acts. These obligations and duties have been imposed in order to protect the child's right to education by seeking to ensure the child's attendance at school in a fit state to benefit from education.[11]

The debate continues into the 1990s, following the new legal requirements of the Education Reform Act 1988 and the Children Act 1989,[12] but as we show in Chapters 7 and 8, many of these basic support services are now very much at the margins of provision.

TOWARDS EQUALITY OF EDUCATIONAL OPPORTUNITY

The second stage centres on the question of equality of educational opportunity – *equality of access* – to education. In particular, it concerns the long and still unresolved debate about the nature of secondary education. Initially, the aim of a broad general education for all beyond the compulsory stage remained little more than an ideal kept alive by part of the labour movement.[13] In practice, expansion in secondary education continued the grammar school pattern for a minority of pupils who were considered able to profit from it. This required some kind of selective procedure – whether through the award of scholarships and free places, or by the full-blown 11-plus procedures. Selection itself was strongly underpinned by the widely held belief that only a limited number of children would benefit from this form of academic education and clear criteria of educational merit were applied at entry. This in turn depended on the widespread belief in a relatively fixed nature of ability, which could be more or less accurately measured by intelligence tests. Secondary school provision was therefore to be '"equal but different" ... according to measured ability and assumed needs'.[14]

Several developments combined to weaken this consensus in the post-war period. First, there was the failure to develop alternatives to the grammar school. Technical schools were never set up in any numbers and secondary modern schools were never accorded the same prestige or resources as the grammar schools. The result was to increase pressure at 11-plus, widely regarded as the marker of educational success or failure and the critical point in a child's future educational career. This development in turn underlined inequalities and inconsistencies – the huge geographical variation in the number of grammar school places, inequalities between the number of places for boys and girls, variations in the age group for transfer (a problem for mobile families) and varied and inconsistent methods of selection from one area to another. Research also demonstrated the unreliability of the 11-plus assessment procedure for borderline candidates, where boundary decisions on allocation – whether you got a grammar school place or not – could be based on minute and meaningless variations in the test score.[15]

But perhaps the most important challenge to this system came from the strong and continuing links between the selection procedures and social background. Grammar schools continued to recruit a disproportionately high percentage of their intake from non-manual backgrounds. Halsey, Heath and Ridge's research shows that among groups of boys born between 1913 and 1952, more than two-thirds from higher, non-manual backgrounds consistently obtained selective secondary places, as against only a quarter of children from working class backgrounds.[16]

At the same time, the notion of a fixed and stable intelligence also came under sustained attack, with a growing emphasis on the social and environmental factors that influenced educational attainment.

Measured against the widely accepted social goal of 'equality of educational opportunity', the selective secondary system was found wanting. The pressure for a more comprehensive form of secondary education for all gathered pace from the mid-1960s to the mid-1970s. Just over one-third (34.4 per cent) of those in public sector secondary education in England in 1971 attended comprehensive schools, while just under one-fifth (18.4 per cent) went to grammar schools. A decade later, the proportion attending comprehensive schools had risen to nearly 90 per cent (including middle schools) and the proportion in grammar schools had dropped sharply to just over 3 per cent. Grammar school numbers began to rise again in the late 1980s. With the arrival of 'opting out', grant-maintained schools – which were already catering for 8 per cent of secondary pupils in

1993 – represent a return to the possibilities of selection. Chapter 5 discusses what this may mean for children from low-income families in poorer areas. However, the key point for selection has now shifted upwards from age 11-plus to 16 and even 18-plus.

EQUALISING EDUCATIONAL OUTCOMES AND RESULTS

> Schools in deprived areas should be given priority in many respects. The first step must be to raise the school with low standards to the national average, the second quite deliberately to make them better.
>
> Plowden Report, para 148

The concern for equality of educational opportunity quickly led to further developments. The view of James Coleman, whose massive US government study of equality of educational opportunity in 1966 focused on the black-white gap in educational achievement, was that equality of opportunity could not be defined simply in terms of equality of *access* to resources, but should be measured in terms of the *effectiveness* of those resources in equalising the overall pattern of results from unequal starting points.[17] The important goal was *equality of outcomes* for different social and ethnic groups.

The idea of additional resources targeted on particular groups or areas was hardly new. Nor was the idea of providing extra teachers, better buildings or even paying teachers extra to work in difficult areas unknown. But these ideas came together powerfully in Britain in the 1960s, particularly in the proposal of the Plowden Committee on Primary Education for the creation of Educational Priority Areas (EPAs).

The concept of EPAs capitalised on the belief that education could make a major difference to reducing social inequality (derived to an extent from the heady optimism of the early stages of the American 'War on Poverty', with its heavy emphasis on education).

The ideas stemming from the Plowden Report of 'educational priority' (later, 'social priority') ran through much educational thinking of this period; not just on policy, but on curriculum development, school organisation (in the emphasis on community schooling in disadvantaged areas) and teacher training. Even Mrs Thatcher's 1972 White Paper on nursery expansion[18] included a clear priority for areas of social disadvantage.

The Plowden proposals for EPAs were never implemented on any scale, but they had a significant influence on policy thinking beyond education. The idea of identifying areas of social disadvantage spread first to the Urban Programme launched in the late 1960s[19] and then to the series of inner city programmes lasting up to the introduction of the Single Regeneration Budget in 1994. These later developments took over the baton of social reform as education's claims to be at the centre of social policy flagged in the more pessimistic climate of the late 1970s. In education, the more pressing concerns were considered to be the sharply rising unemployment among young people, educational standards and the relevance of the school curriculum to employment needs. This emphasis was most brutally articulated by Callaghan, the then prime minister, in his 'Ruskin' speech:

> there is no virtue in producing socially well-adjusted members of society who are unemployed because they do not have the skills.[20]

Broad concern with social disadvantage also gave way in the latter part of the 1970s to a sharper focus on particular groups – children with special educational needs in the Warnock Committee's report (1978), ethnic minorities in the Swann Committee's report (1985) and the so-called 'bottom 40 per cent ' in the Lower Attaining Pupils Project (LAPP). It was not until the 1990s that policy attention turned again to the general problems of social disadvantage, a strong theme in the National Commission on Education's report[21] and the 1993 HMI study of urban areas.[22]

FROM SOCIAL ENGINEERING TO MARKET FORCES

> ... by specifying that the allocation of delegated budgets should be primarily pupil-led, the Education Reform Act 1988 ensured that parental choice directly influences individual schools – the more pupils a school attracts, the larger its budget.
>
> *Choice and Diversity*, 1992, para 1.17, Cm 2021

Since the mid-1980s schools and education have experienced an unprecedented rate of legislative change.[23] These policies explicitly rejected the aim of equalising outcomes as unacceptable 'social engineering', and very effectively drew a thick line under previous developments. As Silver and Silver note in their account of poverty and educational policy:

> what began as a history of a highly significant thread in twentieth-century educational and social policy internationally, seemed... to have become by the second half of the 1980s, almost an obituary.[24]

Broadly, these reforms can be grouped into two main types. First come the centralising changes that have increased the power of government and its direct involvement in educational provision, replacing the long-standing 'partnership' between central government, local authorities and schools. This is seen most dramatically in the introduction of the statutory national curriculum and assessment system following the 1988 Education Reform Act. It is encapsulated in the first two clauses of the Education Act 1993, which detail the Secretary of State's general responsibilities over education in England and Wales. It is seen, too, in the national system of four-yearly school inspections, instituted following the Education (Schools) Act 1992, and in the annual 'league tables' of secondary school examination results. It is seen in the enormous number of powers taken by successive Secretaries of State over almost every aspect of the educational system.

But, second, there are the changes that have apparently decentralised power within the system, reducing the influence of local education authorities and possibly leading to their demise. The emphasis on parental choice was first tentatively expressed in the Education Act 1980, but then spelt out as a central element in later policy, and particularly in the Parent's Charter. Under the 1988 Act, local management of schools (LMS) requires local authorities to devolve increasing proportions of the total budget to schools, thereby reducing the power of the local authority to deliver services independently, and linking a school's funding very directly to the number of pupils on roll. Both the 1986 and 1988 Acts substantially increased the responsibilities of individual school governing bodies. Further, there was provision under the 1988 Act for schools to 'opt out' of local authority control and become grant maintained (GM). This became a central focus of the 1993 Act. The goal was to increase 'choice and diversity' by encouraging schools to opt out. The national Funding Agency for Schools (FAS) becomes involved in the planning of local provision once 10 per cent of pupils are in GM schools. And ultimately, when the proportion reaches 75 per cent, the FAS takes over responsibility from the LEA. The development of 'City Technology Colleges' (CTCs) also formed part of the policy of creating diversity.

Taken together, these changes are deliberately designed to shift the school system towards a more market-based approach, with the school resembling a small business.[25] The individual school has to respond to its 'local market' by attracting parental support and choice. Schools which are successful and increase or hold their market share are likely to flourish; those with a declining share will go to the wall. The power of the local authority to intervene to protect weaker schools is reduced through both loss of control over school funding and the possibility that other schools will opt out if they disagree with local authority decisions. Increasingly tight central government control over local authority spending has further reduced scope for independent action.

But it is not a free market. Schools' and governors' greater autonomy is highly restricted by a much tighter framework of control laid down by central government. Nor do schools have leverage over the total size of their budgets, though they are free to raise their own funds if they can. Parents, too, may theoretically have greater choice, but this can be exercised only if there is space available or, indeed, a choice of local schools at all. If it is a market, it is highly regulated and controlled, even if it is not quite 'engineered'.

One clear casualty of these changes has been the social dimension in education, and not just in policy. First, one consequence of concentrating on the central curriculum objectives of education has been to marginalise those services and resources with a broader social and welfare purpose. Where they have been retained, they play an increasingly 'residual' rather than central role, as we show in Chapters 7 and 8; in other cases the service has been reorganised into a different setting (for example, the old school health service), or reshaped to more traditional ends (as with the educational welfare service). The dominant focus of the national curriculum has also tended to squeeze out some of the broader themes concerned with the all-round development of the individual: at best, these may be retained as 'cross-curricular' themes.

Second, the idea of a market puts the onus for success or failure on the *individual* pupil, parent or school. It is up to them to maximise their opportunity. In principle, the statutory framework, assessment and regulation lay down equal conditions for all. The massive differences between different social groups remain, but they can now be 'individualised' out of sight.

Many of these ideas for 'educational markets' are borrowed from the US. Yet many Americans continue to emphasise education's social dimension alongside the necessary partnership between the education system, schools and the community. This belief was forcefully spelt out by Tom Sobol, Commissioner of Education for New York State, at the North of England Education Conference in January 1994:

> We know that you cannot separate the way children learn from the way children live, and that therefore our schools must help to meet the needs of 'the whole child'. Boys and girls who are sick, hungry, or afraid are not students – they are sick, hungry and fearful boys and girls. There is no use wringing hands about the decline of the family and deteriorating neighbourhoods, nor in debating what the role of the school *should* be. The fact is, if you want them to learn, you'd better help them, feed them, make them feel more secure, and give them someone to talk to ... We really do believe that 'it takes a whole village to raise a child'.[26]

Sobol's message takes us back directly to our starting point with the introduction of 'penny dinners' and school clothing in this country. Recent studies on the serious consequences of low income for the health and welfare of young children[27] sharply remind us that these barriers to learning are still in place at the end of the 20th century. A policy for equal opportunity and high standards in education which ignored these factors would be based on a bogus prospectus.

NOTES

1. The 1870 Act allowed for part-time attendance for those who needed to continue with paid employment. The 1876 Elementary Education Act made full-time attendance compulsory for all children.
2. W E Forster, *Hansard*, 17 February 1870.
3. The school meals service was taken over by the education authorities in 1906 and the school health service in 1907. The school leaving age was raised to 14 by the 1918 Education Act.
4. G A N Lowndes, *The Silent Social Revolution: an account of the expansion of public education in England and Wales 1895-1965*, OUP, 1969, p170.
5. Education (Provision of Meals) Act 1906, s3.
6. They also supplied 'data for the poverty surveys of the time' and called 'for the improvement of housing conditions which were believed to be a basic cause of ill-health, crime and poor school attendance'; K Macmillan, *Education Welfare: strategy and structure*, Longman, 1977, pp27-8.
7. Quoted in J Wardhaugh, 'Regulating truancy: the role of the education welfare service', *Sociological Review*, 38, pp735-64.
8. The Plowden Committee, reporting in 1967, described the role in both

legal and welfare terms thus: 'securing regular attendance ... acting as the liaison officer between home, school and the local authority and agencies for the welfare of children ... arranging for the provision of school meals and clothing to necessitous cases' (Plowden Committee, *Children and Their Primary Schools: a report of the Central Advisory Council for Education*, HMSO, 1967, paras 217-18). The Seebohm Committee, while acknowledging similar functions for the education welfare service, argued for a new education social work service as part of the proposed new social work departments (Seebohm Report, *Report of the Committee on Local Authority and Allied Personal Social Services*, Cmnd 3703, HMSO, 1968, paras 223 ff). The Ralphs Committee, on the other hand, argued that the education welfare officer's social work functions 'should be performed within the educational system', once again repeating the welfare role of education, 'that children are able to benefit to the full from whatever educational opportunities may be offered to them' (Ralphs Report, *The Role of Training of Education Welfare Officers*, HMSO, 1973).

9. Department of Education and Science (DES), *The Education Welfare Service: an HMI enquiry in eight LEAs*, HMSO, 1984.
10. DES, *School Attendance and Education Welfare Services*, Circular 2/86, DES, 1986.
11. DES, *The Education Welfare Service, op cit*, HMSO, para 59.
12. J Wardhaugh, 'Absent without leave: state responses to school non-attendance', *International Studies in Sociology of Education*, 1, pp209-23. W S Rogers and J Roche, *The Children Act 1989: a guide for the Education Service*, Open University, 1991.
13. B Simon, *Education and the Social Order: 1940-1990*, Lawrence and Wishart, 1991.
14. J Mortimore and T Blackstone, *Disadvantage and Education*, Heinemann, 1982, p5.
15. J E Floud, A H Halsey and F M Martin, *Social Class and Educational Opportunity*, Heinemann, 1956; A H Halsey and J E Floud,'Intelligence tests, social class and selection for secondary schools', *British Journal of Sociology*, 3(3), 1957; J Karabel and A H Halsey, *Power and Ideology in Education*, Oxford University Press, 1977.
16. A H Halsey, A Heath and J M Ridge, *Origins and Destinations*, Oxford University Press, 1980, p63.
17. J S Coleman *et al*, *Equality of Educational Opportunity*, Harvard University Press, 1969.
18. DES, *Education: a framework for expansion*, HMSO, 1972; DES, *Nursery Education*, Circular 2/73, 1973.
19. The Urban Programme was started in 1968 by the Labour Government under Harold Wilson, prompted by concern for social and ethnic problems following Enoch Powell's 'rivers of blood' speech. The Community Development Project, the Comprehensive Community

Programmes, Partnership Authorities, Programme Authorities, New Programme Authorities, Task Forces, Inner Area Programmes, Urban Development Grants and Programmes, Urban Renewal Grants, City Action Teams, Enterprise Boards, etc, followed in the 1970s and 1980s.

20. *Times Educational Supplement*, 22 October 1976.
21. National Commission on Education, *Learning to Succeed: a radical look at education today and a strategy for the future*, Heinemann, 1993.
22. Office for Standards in Education, *Access and Achievement in Urban Education*, HMSO, 1993.
23. J Sallis, *Free for All? A brief history of state education including summaries of all recent legislation*, CASE, 1994. This provides a useful summary of educational legislation.
24. H Silver and P Silver, *An Educational War on Poverty: American and British policy making 1960-1980*, Cambridge University Press, 1991, p9.
25. This language is explicit in discussion of the CTCs, for example (see G Whitty, T Edwards and S Gewirtz, *Specialisation and Choice in Urban Education: the City Technology College experiment*, Routledge, 1993).
26. T Sobol, *Building on Diversity*. Speech to the North of England Education Conference, 7 January 1994.
27. R G Wilkinson, *Unfair Shares*, Barnardos, 1994; V Kumar, *Poverty and Inequality in the UK*, National Children's Bureau, 1993.

3 Education and social inequality revisited

Equality not of opportunity, *but of* outcome. *This was the mania that condemned children to fall short of their potential; that treated them as if they were identical – or must be made to be so. A mania that undermined common sense values in schools, rejected proven teaching methods, debased standards – or disposed of them altogether. A canker in our education system which spread from the Sixties on, and deprived great cohorts of our children of the opportunities they deserved.*

John Major, Speech to the Centre for Policy Studies, 1991

... the working class child has had increased absolute chances of going on into some form of higher education ... But class inequalities, measured in relative terms, have apparently remained stable for the past three generations.

A H Halsey, 'Trends in access and equity in higher education', *Oxford Review of Education*, 19(2), 1993

In the 1960s and 1970s it was hardly necessary to justify the importance of the link between education and social background. A prominent theme in social research from the 1950s onwards, it was one used by governments of both persuasions to support the gradual move to comprehensive secondary schooling. It formed an increasingly significant part of the major educational commissions of the period (Crowther, Newsom, Robbins, Plowden), which together provided a detailed and damning social audit of the relative chances of educational success for children from different social backgrounds – from primary school through to higher education. These and other studies underlined the way that broader social inequalities influenced children's educational progress at all points. But they were also, importantly, a message of hope. If the effect of social factors could be reduced by the right educational policies and programmes, then the result would give a boost to overall standards and release untapped potential.

This theme was by no means restricted to this country. By the time of the Plowden Report on primary education in 1967, attention had turned to the most disadvantaged groups and areas. With its call for the creation of Educational Priority Areas (EPAs) and additional funding for the 2 per cent, rising to 10 per cent, of the most disadvantaged areas, Plowden was strongly influenced by the American 'War on Poverty'. This had placed education at the centre of its strategy, particularly through the federal 'Headstart' programme of pre-school expansion in poor neighbourhoods. And it was the American, James Coleman – hardly a radical – who drew attention to the importance of educational outcomes and results in assessing equality of educational opportunity. This did *not* mean making everyone 'identical', but rather equalising the relative chances of children from different social backgrounds, or at least reducing some of the grosser inequalities.

These objectives continued to influence educational policy in many countries and are again returning to centre stage. Thus New York State, which has some of the sharpest extremes of wealth and poverty, has set an explicit target for its 'New Compact for Learning' in the 1990s – the eradication of overall differences in educational achievement by students from different social and ethnic backgrounds.[1] Yet in Britain by the end of the 1980s, in a new form of political correctness, the relationship between educational performance and social conditions had become almost a proscribed topic in public policy debate.

There are several reasons why this should be so. First, there is a justifiable reaction to what had become almost an orthodoxy in educational thinking, and a central feature of many teacher training courses – the emphasis on social factors in educational performance. What began as a message of hope became instead an easily available and circular excuse for poor performance and low expectations: 'they fail because they are socially disadvantaged'.

The view that 'low expectations' – predominantly of teachers, but also by pupils and parents themselves – were the *prime* cause of under-achievement in socially disadvantaged areas became a dominant explanation of poor performance, for example in HMI reports in the 1980s. This view was also sometimes used to justify the very low profile given to data showing wide differences in performance on social, ethnic or gender grounds. Merely to draw attention to these shortfalls could further reinforce low expectations.

Second, there was a clear political rejection of 'social engineering' and a belief that the emphasis on equality was itself directly responsible for low standards by 'levelling down'. As with other areas of social policy, the emphasis was to be on *individual* responsibility rather than on social factors. It was up to individual children, their parents or schools to achieve success. The fact that some children from highly disadvantaged backgrounds were successful was enough to close the door on further argument. While social factors continued to be used – for example, in resource allocation to local authorities – there was much less public charting of these social and educational inequalities, although some local authorities continued to emphasise the continuing importance of factors such as race, gender, social class and low income in educational performance.

The third reason is more technical and has to do with research methods for measuring school effectiveness. It is now broadly accepted that 'value added' – that is, the *progress* that pupils make during schooling – is the fairest way of gauging *school effectiveness*. This means taking account of starting points to see how much impact the school makes. But the emphasis on 'progress' can draw attention away from the actual position at start and finish. As Peter Mortimore and colleagues pointed out in their study of junior schools in London, school factors are most important when it comes to explaining different rates of progress, but social factors remain a major element in explaining both where children start and where they end up.[2]

Together these reasons have combined to turn attention away from the link between social inequality and educational performance. And yet to ignore the problem is not to make it go away.

The Feiffer cartoon (page 28) is not just a question of words. Each term carries with it some explanation of the reasons for such educational failure – whether in the environment, specific social conditions, childrearing patterns, the school or school system, the wider opportunity structure of society, or a combination of them all.

In their comprehensive review of research on the 'cycle of deprivation', Rutter and Madge reject the term 'deprivation', concluding that:

> the word almost functions as a projective test in which each person reads into the concept his own biases and prejudices, regardless of how the word has been used...[3]

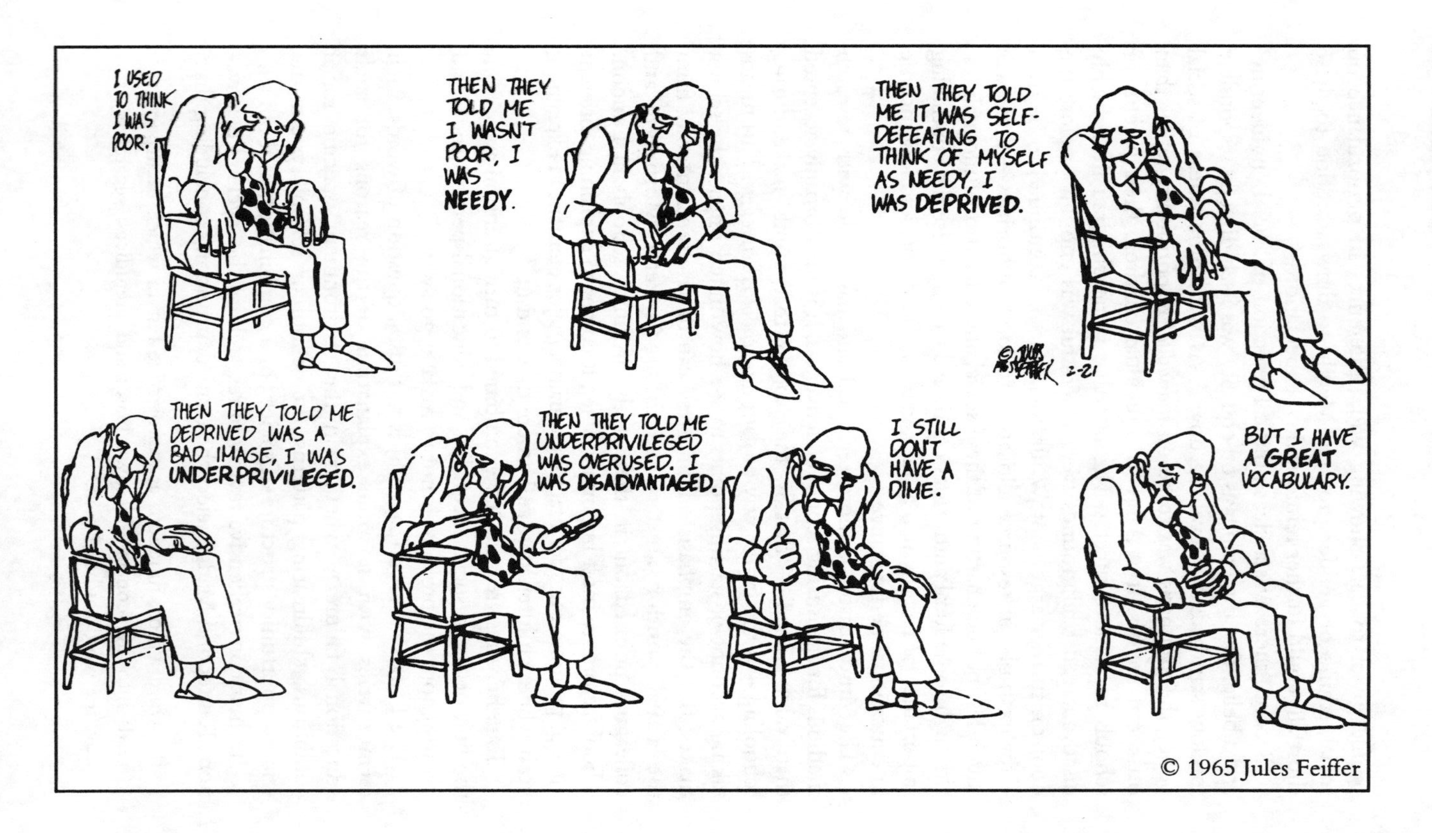
I USED TO THINK I WAS POOR.
THEN THEY TOLD ME I WASN'T POOR, I WAS NEEDY.
THEN THEY TOLD ME IT WAS SELF-DEFEATING TO THINK OF MYSELF AS NEEDY, I WAS DEPRIVED.
THEN THEY TOLD ME DEPRIVED WAS A BAD IMAGE, I WAS UNDERPRIVILEGED.
THEN THEY TOLD ME UNDERPRIVILEGED WAS OVERUSED. I WAS DISADVANTAGED.
I STILL DON'T HAVE A DIME.
BUT I HAVE A GREAT VOCABULARY.

In its place, they substitute the term 'disadvantage' with its broader and more neutral meaning. The term can encompass both material conditions and family, social and economic relationships. It also firmly reinforces the idea of *relative* chances, rather than concentrating on absolute conditions. The term also 'fits' the now much more fractured nature of the social structure, with increasing numbers of children from households outside the labour market.

SOCIAL DISADVANTAGE AND EDUCATIONAL PERFORMANCE

Almost since quantitative measurement of educational performance began, systematic low levels of performance or under-achievement by particular social groups have been revealed. This pattern concerns both educational performance at any given level and persistence into the higher and more selective levels of the educational system. *Group* under-achievement (significantly below average performance by the group) should be distinguished from *individual* under-achievement. While some of the inequalities in educational attainment have changed quite radically over a 20-year period – certainly those linked to gender and possibly for some of the ethnic minority groups – those linked to social and economic inequalities have remained stubbornly resistant to change.

EXPLANATIONS

Why should this be so? There has been no shortage of attempts to explain these persistent differences. These have drawn on three very different sets of evidence: on social and economic conditions, on the patterns of socialisation within the family and home, and on the quality and effectiveness of educational provision.

THE EFFECTS OF SOCIAL BACKGROUND

The first perspective draws on the extensive body of research on educational performance and social class, which locates educational disadvantage squarely in:

the broader context of the relationship between social class, educational performance and equality of opportunity.[4]

It is these adverse social and economic conditions in income, housing, job opportunities and the local environment which depress performance. Long-term follow-up studies of children born in 1947, 1958 and 1970 provide conclusive evidence of a wide – and sometimes widening – gap in educational performance among children from different social backgrounds.[5] Data from the 1958 cohort provides supporting evidence for the variable impact of social and economic disadvantage.

Individuals move in and out of 'social disadvantage', as Essen and Wedge's longitudinal study of children aged 11 and 16 shows. When they distinguished three groups (either disadvantaged at 11 and 16, or at one but not both ages), they found that those who were disadvantaged at 11 but not at 16 did slightly better than the other two groups, but still had a significantly poorer performance than the non-disadvantaged group. Children with one or two adversities (the 'mid-group') fell between the ordinary and disadvantaged groups. The effects of disadvantage seemed to be experienced more or less equally by those with relatively high or low initial attainment levels. The authors conclude:

> It is not solely the low attainment levels of the disadvantaged on entering secondary school which are associated with their limited progress, as the relatively high attainers make just as poor progress. It is their disadvantaged status itself which seems to be associated with their poor progress, and this is so even for those no longer disadvantaged at 16.[6]

Their findings on the progress of 'bright' children from disadvantaged backgrounds also demonstrate the impact of social conditions. The authors point out that the scores of disadvantaged children from homes

> with the advantages of parents who were well educated and interested in further education for their children were not as high as might have been expected … it may be that the daily pressures of financial, housing and family difficulties are so great that the positive ambitions and education of the parents are less influential in terms of the children's level of success at school.[7]

EARLY SOCIALISATION IN THE HOME

The evidence that poor educational performance was already established at an early age – certainly by the time children entered school – focused attention on early experience and particularly the mother-child relationship. Studies concentrated on patterns of early socialisation, particularly the child's linguistic development, the mother's control styles, and more broadly the educational support and climate of the home. The so-called 'deficit' model of the 'disadvantaged child' which emerged when these studies were put together had a substantial impact on many of the American pre-school programmes of the 1960s and 1970s, and on similar work in Britain in the 1970s. It undoubtedly led to a heavy emphasis on early linguistic development to 'compensate' the child for any alleged lack of this and other experiences in the home background.[8] Lack of skills was taken as 'a deficit' and evidence of 'pathological' conditions. But in some cases such behaviour could well be a perfectly appropriate response: for example, parents may reasonably restrict young children's play or curiosity in what are potentially dangerous environments.[9]

Tizard and her colleagues[10] made use of taped information recorded both in the home and in a nursery school for pre-school girls from working-class and middle-class backgrounds. They point to the extensive and often sophisticated verbal and reasoning skills displayed by the working-class group at home, contrasted with the much more restricted performance of the same group at school. Many of the skills that the 'verbal deprivation' thesis would lead us to expect to be absent from the home were in fact discovered in the conversations between mother and child. But by contrast, the interactions between the nursery staff and the children in the nursery were much less rich, and – even more striking – the working class children tended to receive less verbal contact, stimulation and encouragement from staff than did the middle class children.[11]

EDUCATIONAL DISADVANTAGE

The third perspective locates the problem firmly within the educational system, which through either its formal structures or its informal operation fails to provide the appropriate educational climate for children from socially disadvantaged backgrounds. In part this third strand draws on the other two – the influence of the peer group, the gap between the home and school, and the low or inappropriate expectations of parents or teachers. But the emphasis is on the response of the school or educational system. School effectiveness research has increasingly demonstrated that schools do make a difference and has begun to pin down the factors that make some schools more effective than others.

None of the three perspectives on its own appears to provide a complete explanation of educational disadvantage. The most telling criticism of that based on social conditions is that it fails to explain why *some* children from very disadvantaged backgrounds are educationally successful. If social factors are so important, why are their effects apparently so variable? The objection most frequently raised to the psychological tradition was almost the mirror image of this point. If the explanation for educational disadvantage is merely a matter of how individuals learn or problems within the family stemming from the mother-child relationship, or other early experiences, why is the pattern of educational performance so predictably regular if we look across social and economic divisions? Again, targeting the educational system fails to provide a complete answer, as some of the differences emerge before children enter school, although they widen during the school years.[12]

Follow-up studies of progress made by children from extremely disadvantaged circumstances are beginning to present a picture of how these different factors fit together and affect children's educational progress over time. Studies such as the 20-year follow-up of children who experienced special pre-school programmes in the US show that there is no straightforward linear pattern of cause and effect.[13] While initial advantages in children's performance when they entered school 'washed out' after a few years in school, other effects on school competence and children's motivation seem longer-lasting. One explanation is that early intervention programmes both help children at entry to school and promote increased parental support for their education by establishing a cycle of positive reinforcement between child and parents.[14] Their successful progress came as much from *avoiding* some of the problems and pitfalls encountered by children who had not had the pre-school boost.[15]

This suggests a rather more dynamic picture of the way social disadvantage operates, not as a fixed handicap which inhibits progress, but rather as a series of events that may intervene to check or undermine progress throughout the child's education. These would include ill-health, financial pressures on the family, family stress and breakdown. Such events are statistically more likely to happen to children from disadvantaged backgrounds, where families may have fewer resources to cope. Additionally, the increased concentration of such families and children in particular areas puts increasing pressures on schools, and limits their capacity to offer an effective education for *all* their children.

NOTES

1. New York State Department of Education, *New Compact for Learning*, 1991.
2. P Mortimore, P Sammons and L Stoll, *School Matters: the junior years*, Open Books, 1983.
3. M Rutter and N Madge, *Cycles of Disadvantage: a review of research*, Heinemann, 1976, p2.
4. J Mortimore and T Blackstone, *Disadvantage and Education*, Gower, 1982, p5.
5. J W B Douglas, *The Home and the School*, McGibbon and Kee, 1964; J W B Douglas, J M Ross and H R Simpson, *All Our Future: a longitudinal study of secondary education*, Peter Davies, 1968; R Davie, N R Butler and H Goldstein, *From Birth to Seven: a report of the National Child Development Study (NCDS)*, Longman, 1972; A F Osborn, N R Butler and A C Morris, *The Social Life of Britain's Five Year Olds*, Routledge and Kegan Paul, 1984; A F Osborn and J E Milbank, *The Effects of Early Education*, Clarendon Press, 1987.
6. J Essen and P Wedge, *Continuities in Childhood Deprivation*, Gower, 1982, p126.
7. *Ibid*, p117.
8. These studies are reviewed by Rutter and Madge, *op cit* (pp224ff) and Mortimore and Blackstone, *op cit*.
9. This argument is put forward in H Wilson and G W Herbert, *Parents and Children in the Inner City*, Routledge and Kegan Paul, 1978.
10. B Tizard and M Hughes, *Young Children Learning: talking and thinking at home and at school*, Fontana, 1984.
11. However, a weakness of this study is that it is based on a small sample of girls only, and the material conditions of the home and the tested level of the children do not suggest a highly disadvantaged group.
12. See, for example, Osborn and Milbank, *op cit*.
13. K Sylva, 'The importance of early learning on children's later development', in C Ball, *Start Right: the importance of early learning*, Royal Society for the Encouragement of Arts, Manufacture and Commerce, 1994.
14. I Lazar and R Darlington, *Lasting Effects of Early Education: a report from the Consortium for Longitudinal Studies*, Monographs of the Society for Research in Child Development, No. 195, vol. 47, Nos 2-3, University

of Chicago Press, 1982.

15. L J Schweinhart, H V Barnes and D P Weikart, *Significant Benefits: the High/Scope Perry Preschool Study through age 27*, Monographs of the High/Scope Educational Foundation No. 10, High/Scope Press, 1993.

II
Education: the new market system

The shift from a 'public service' ethos to 'market forces' in education gathered pace after 1988, when the Education Reform Act introduced local management of schools and the possibility of schools 'opting out' from local education authority control – both intended to reduce the power of local authorities and increase parental choice and control over their children's education.

In the next three chapters we explore these changes and their impact on disadvantaged children and families. In Chapters 5 and 6 we illustrate what parental choice means in practice. But we start in Chapter 4 with resources and resource allocation. The last 30 years have seen two major educational restructurings: the Labour Government's introduction of comprehensive education through Circular 10/65, and the Conservative Government's 1988 Education Reform Act. It has often been pointed out that while the former relied mainly on encouragement and exhortation, the latter changed the entire basis of educational funding. Where money flows, change will follow: that perhaps is the sternest lesson of the market.

II
Education: the new market system

[illegible]

[illegible]

4 Changing resource allocation

Nothing cheers me up more, after nearly a year at the Department of Education, than to note the lingering death of the argument that used to dominate the education debate about how much money is flowing into the school system.

John Patten, then Secretary of State for Education,
The Independent, 5 April 1993[1]

This year I find myself cutting back on essentials to try and save money because I know I am going to be short in the next financial year.
...I have a simple dichotomy of employing staff or buying educational supplies. Both are vital...

Primary heads in Trafford, December 1993[2]

Mr Patten's comments reflect the Government's strategy of successfully 'unhooking' the debate about educational quality and standards from questions about the level of resources and funding for education. Where debate has been encouraged, it has been about the *means* by which funds are allocated – for example, devolving budgets to schools – rather than the *amount*. Starting from the research evidence on the apparent lack of any clear links between resource inputs in education and educational results, the conclusion falsely drawn has sometimes been that the level and distribution of resources do not really matter at all. If high spending areas or schools produce no better results than those that spend less, runs the argument, why spend more?

Clearly, on the ground, the experience in schools has been very different, but demands by schools for additional resources have often made little impact at the national level, being dismissed by government as inevitable 'special pleading'. But there are now, in the mid-1990s, many signs that this is changing. Questions of resource allocation are again at the centre of educational debate[3] and likely to be the dominant issue over the next few years. In research, too, the links between educational resourcing and results are being re-examined on the grounds that an over-mechanical 'input-output' analysis has obscured the real picture. The level and distribution of funding are again seen to be critical ingredients in the debate on educational standards and quality, particularly for economically and socially disadvantaged areas.

For these reasons we make no apology for starting with the central question of funding in education. In this chapter we set out recent evidence on three related questions:

- How much is spent on school education? Is this rising or falling?
- Is funding fairly distributed?
- What are the main sources of funding for schools? How are these changing?

CPAG supporters may have most interest in the fair distribution of resources, but the *overall amount* cannot be ignored. There may be only cold comfort in equality of resources if the amount distributed is inadequate. The financing of education is a complex and difficult topic. Inevitably, what follows means grappling with some of this complexity.

OVERALL LEVELS OF EXPENDITURE ON SCHOOLS

CURRENT EXPENDITURE OVERALL

The Department for Education's *Statistical Bulletin 4/94*[4] concludes that overall levels of current expenditure on maintained schools in England have increased in real terms (that is, taking inflation into account) by 24 per cent in the period 1979/80 to 1991/92 (36 per cent at primary, 12 per cent at secondary level). At first sight, then, there appear to be few grounds for complaint. However, first impressions can be misleading – these figures merit close inspection and comparison with data from other sources.

First, if we use Chartered Institute of Public Finance Accountants (CIPFA) data on LEA expenditure in England and Wales since

1980/81, we see a rather more modest growth. Thus, overall expenditure by LEAs on maintained schools rose by 18 per cent in the period 1980/81 to 1992/93, taking account of general inflation. Nursery/primary and special schools, with increases of 35 per cent and 39 per cent, fared better than secondary schools, where the increase was under 3 per cent for the 12-year period. Part of the increase at primary level is undoubtedly explained by an increase in expenditure on under-fives over the decade. LEA expenditure on under-fives increased from under 10 per cent of the primary total in 1979/80 to nearly 20 per cent by 1992/93.

Second, to take 1978/79 as the starting point distorts the picture. If we go back to 1975 when national educational expenditure was at its peak, the increase in spending on schools has been only marginal – about 2 per cent, taking into account general inflation, by 1990. In fact, overall spending declined to the mid-1980s and then rose again in the late 1980s.[5]

Third, the adjustment used to take into account the effects of inflation makes a significant difference. If we use the CIPFA 'education cost index', which takes account of teacher salaries and other educational costs, rather than the general inflation index, the picture changes again. Taking this index into account, overall expenditure has varied little between 1980/81 and 1992/93. However, total secondary expenditure *falls by* about 14 per cent and nursery and primary expenditure *rises by* about 13 per cent over the same period. Using this cost adjustment shows the real impact at school level of *maintaining* quality – that is, employing the same number of teachers – from year to year.

PER PUPIL EXPENDITURE

Of course, over much of this period the overall number of pupils fell sharply at both primary and secondary level (by 13 per cent between 1980/81-1991/92). Unless costs fall at the same rate, there is an inevitable increase in per pupil expenditure. These changes take no account of diseconomies of scale, when numbers fall, nor any changes in the age distribution of pupils (for example, more under-fives or more post-16, where costs are significantly higher).

The DFE statistics on expenditure *per pupil* for the period 1979/80 to 1991/92 show rises which seem even more striking than rises in overall expenditure; 50 per cent at nursery/primary level, 55 per cent at secondary and 100 per cent for special schools. Again, CIPFA figures for 1980/81-1992/93 show rather more modest increases per pupil than the DFE and, if the CIPFA education cost index is used, these are reduced to 21 per cent at primary level and 23 per cent at secondary.

As figure 4.1 (opposite) shows, per pupil costs at secondary level peaked in 1990 but have since begun to drop quite sharply to levels last seen in 1987/88, as overall numbers at secondary level have begun to rise again.[6] Primary figures have turned down only in the most recent year's data (1992/93). Most recent estimates suggest these trends will continue.

Spending on schools since 1980/81

- When education costs are taken into account overall spending on schools has hardly changed at all since 1980/81, and has fallen sharply at secondary level.
- Increases in per pupil expenditure were largely the result of LEAs maintaining overall levels of expenditure as pupil numbers fell. As pupil numbers have risen, expenditure per pupil has begun to drop. As a result, pupil-teacher ratios are rising at both primary and secondary level and will continue to rise, unless significantly more resources are devoted to schools.

EXPENDITURE ON SCHOOL BUILDINGS

> The general condition of the fabric of buildings and the state of internal decoration in many [secondary] schools continues to be unsatisfactory.
>
> HM Senior Chief Inspector of Schools, 1991[7]

The pattern for capital expenditure on school buildings is clear. It has fallen steeply and stayed very low. In 1975/76 capital expenditure on schools amounted to nearly 12 per cent of total educational expenditure; by the early 1980s it was down to just 4-5 per cent of current expenditure and has stayed at this level ever since. Organisation for Economic Co-operation and Development (OECD) figures show that public sector capital spending in education in the UK was well below the OECD average.[8] Sustained capital expenditure at this low level shows up in the deteriorating conditions of school buildings and increasing backlog of major and minor works.

Figure 4.1: **Per pupil increase in expenditure: primary and secondary – education cost index**

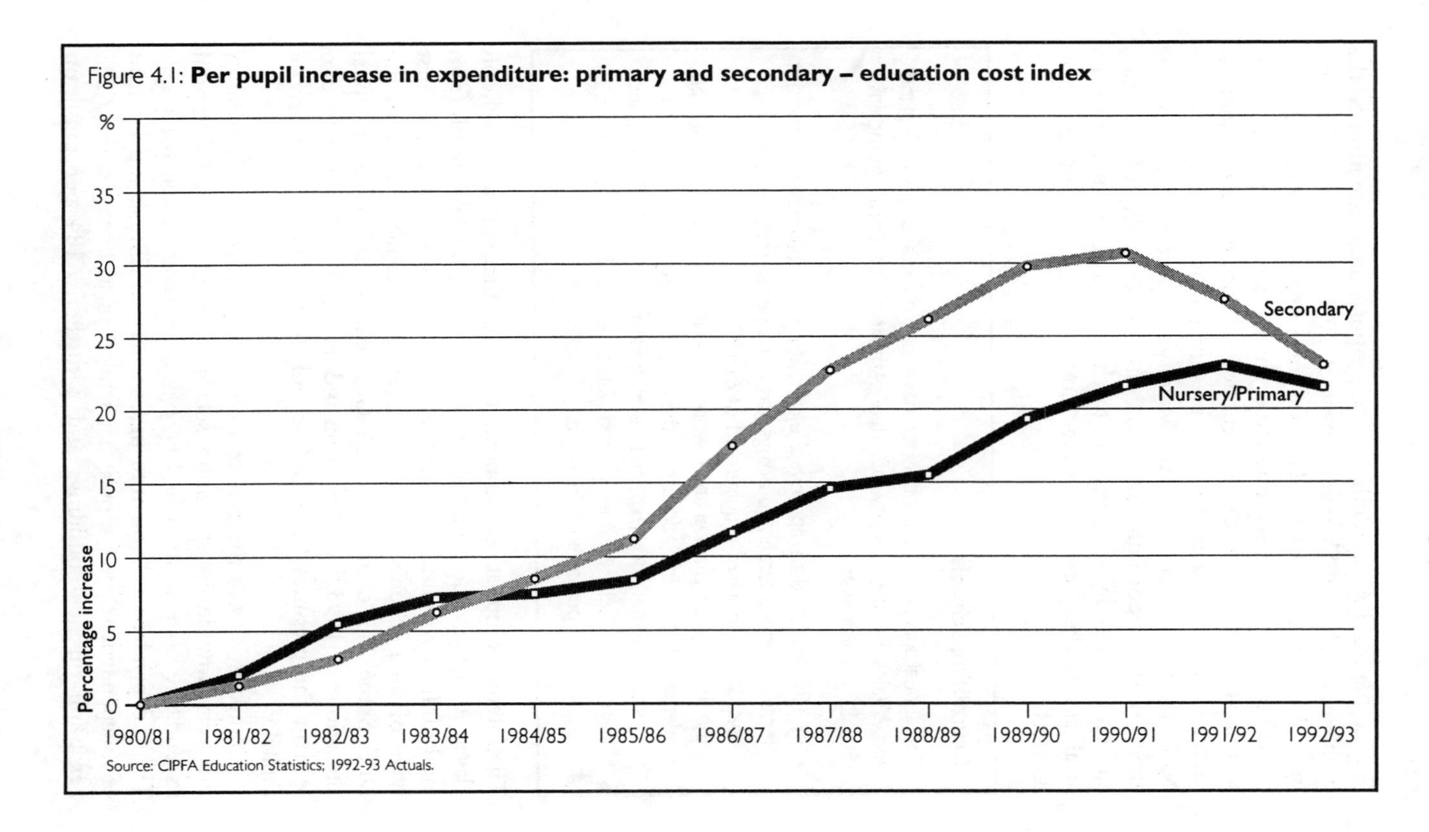

Source: CIPFA Education Statistics; 1992-93 Actuals.

The National Audit Office (NAO) report[9] drew attention to this problem. In the DES's own survey of 1986, the cost of bringing 'school buildings up to standard was estimated to be £2bn at 1987 prices' or more than six times the annual capital expenditure on schools at that time. The causes identified included failure to undertake sufficient routine maintenance to prevent problems developing. The NAO cited evidence from Her Majesty's Inspectors (HMI) on the effects of such poor building conditions, on the quality of education and on the morale of pupils and teachers. In a series of surveys on local authorities, 'problems were most severe in the metropolitan districts'.[10]

Crumbling schools

The annual survey of local authority maintenance expenditure in England and Wales by the Society of Chief Architects of Local Authorities (SCALA) found that:

- in 1991/92 median approved expenditure on maintenance for all local authority education buildings was £7.08 per sq metre of floorspace against an estimated requirement of £18.88;
- the backlog of maintenance work in education would require an average 80 per cent addition to the amount already committed;
- average maintenance expenditure in education in 1990/91 was less than 1 per cent of the insured value of the buildings, against a required 2.5 per cent of the value.

The intense competition and need for capital funding among schools played its part in the initial phase of the opting out of schools from local authority control to grant maintained (GM) status. The first wave of such schools received preference for capital bids from the DFE. Some 217 of the first 255 GM schools had received capital allocations by 1993.[11] Competition and the need for funding are also seen in the pressures from GM schools to be able to raise private capital.[12]

Comparison with the private sector also gives some indication of the very low level of public sector investment. LEAs' capital expenditure on education in 1992/93 was roughly £100 per pupil. The Independent Schools Information Service (ISIS) annual census of independent schools shows that schools in its survey spent £283 per pupil on new buildings and a further £184 per pupil on improvements to buildings and equipment. The total of £468 per pupil in 1993 showed a fall from £513 in 1992.[13]

> **Outdoor Blues**
>
> A National Union of Teachers (NUT) survey of 2,000 schools in England and Wales has shown that 17 per cent of primaries and 8 per cent of secondaries have outside lavatories. Twenty-eight per cent of the secondaries with outside lavatories and 36 per cent of the primaries do not have running water.
>
> *Times Educational Supplement*, 7 February 1992

THE DISTRIBUTION OF RESOURCES

The second question to ask is how fairly these overall resources are distributed to schools. This involves central government allocation to local authorities and, in turn, local authority allocations to schools. Both are essentially block grants determined by explicit formulae. This apparently more rational and open process should, in principle, make it easier to follow how resources are distributed. In practice, the results of such formula allocations have been rather to focus attention on the anomalies between apparently similar schools or LEAs that receive very different levels of funding. In looking at these funding allocations it is important to look at both the criteria used and the *proportion* of the total budget they influence. However finely pitched criteria of social need may be, they will make little impact if they influence only 1 per cent of the budget.

CENTRAL GOVERNMENT ALLOCATION TO LOCAL AUTHORITIES: STANDARD SPENDING ASSESSMENTS

The majority of local authority expenditure is provided by central government grant. This comes in the form of a block grant to the authority as a whole (not just the LEA). The total block grant allocated to each local authority is based on its Standard Spending Assessment (SSA).

The most important ingredient in estimating SSAs is the relevant population figure for each LEA; for example, pupils aged 5-10 for the primary formula. However, from the perspective of those concerned with poverty, the most important element is the Additional Educational Needs (AEN) budget.

What is the Standard Spending Assessment?

The Standard Spending Assessment (SSA) is the amount the government assesses that local authorities need to provide a standard level of services. The SSA is the basis of the central government block grant to local authorities. The SSA for each authority is calculated each year by central government on the basis of detailed formulae for each area of expenditure. There is thus an education SSA and within that, five separate categories (Primary, Secondary, Post-16, under-5, Other), each with its own formula.

Despite these exceedingly detailed assessments by central government, the total transferred is a *block* grant, with no obligation on the local authority to spend according to these detailed assessments. Thus a local authority might receive a notional allocation under the 'under-5' heading as part of its education SSA, but may in fact provide no nursery education at all.

Increasingly, as the expenditure 'cap' on local authority spending has been tightened to a small percentage above the SSA total, an authority's SSA closely determines the absolute level of funding possible. This is particularly true for education, as it is such a large proportion of the total local authority budget (56 per cent of total expenditure in shire counties). How the education SSA (and other SSAs) is worked out is thus critical to local authority expenditure.

ADDITIONAL EDUCATIONAL NEEDS (AEN)

AEN is a variable addition to each local authority's allocation to reflect extra needs; for example, for special educational needs pupils or pupil support costs. The calculation of each LEA's AEN 'index score' is based on indicators of social need. This index is used to allocate a proportion of the total education SSA. Two factors are thus critical – the selection of indicators that make up the AEN index and the proportion of the total budget allocated by this index score.

Prior to 1990 the AEN index was based on six social factors, each given a slightly different weighting. The proportion of the total budget allocated was 10.5 per cent of the total block grant. When the 'poll tax' was introduced, the AEN formula was reviewed and simplified.

The AEN index score in use from April 1990 until April 1994 was based on the percentages of children in three types of household: lone parents; head of household born outside the UK; dependent on income support (IS). The first two were drawn from the 1981 Census. The last item is based on LEA counts provided annually by the DSS. The lone parent and income support items were given a weight of 1.5.

The 1990 change in the AEN index would of itself have had some impact on local authority funding. However, more important was the decision to raise the proportion of the total educational component to be distributed according to the AEN index score for each local authority, to approximately 24 per cent. This had the effect of shifting funds significantly towards areas with high AEN index scores. In a total educational budget of some £16bn in 1990, £4bn was differentially allocated on the basis of the AEN index. In part, these allocations helped to maintain educational expenditure in the LEAs which took over from the Inner London Education Authority, because the AEN index tended to favour inner London.

Inner, and some outer, London boroughs have particularly high AEN index scores because they have proportionately more lone parent households; also, some London boroughs score highly in terms of the proportion of children from non-UK backgrounds. The 1990/91 AEN index ranged from Hackney with the highest (1.54855) to Surrey with the lowest (0.31925). The extremes are hardly surprising. But there are some unexpected results, with Harrow, for example, having higher needs indices than Barnsley; Croydon higher than Sheffield; and Wandsworth and Westminster (which have significant proportions of both poor and well-off families) coming out higher than Liverpool or Knowsley.

Table 4.1 shows some of these anomalies. Basically the formula tended to favour some boroughs in the London area and tip resources away from some declining industrial areas in the North West, North or South Yorkshire. Yet in terms of educational performance, as the table shows, it is often these boroughs, or LEAs, which have very poor educational results. Thus, Harrow LEA has been consistently top or very high in the league of higher grade GCSE results (5 or more grades A-C), whereas Barnsley is much lower. Knowsley, which comes near the bottom of the league in terms of GCSE higher grades, has an AEN index score very similar to that of Ealing. Yet on other measures, for example in terms of social class distribution, Harrow with 44 per cent of its children from higher non-manual backgrounds and 20 per cent from poorer backgrounds is clearly less disadvantaged than Barnsley (with 19 per cent and 41 per cent respectively); with Knowsley much lower than Wandsworth or Ealing.

TABLE 4.1: **Selected AEN Scores and Proportions Gaining Higher Grade GCSEs, 1992**

LEA	AEN Index (higher=more need)	% 16 year old with 5 or more GCSEs grade A-C	% 0-15 from low socio-economic group	% 0-15 from high socio-economic group
Barnsley	0.5004	24.2	41.3	18.8
Harrow	0.56155	46.7	20.0	43.5
Sheffield	0.60505	29.7	34.9	27.4
Croydon	0.6548	38.7	24.4	36.7
Knowsley	0.90365	16.9	51.3	13.1
Ealing	0.9094	27.2	32.4	32.0
Liverpool	0.9647	22.2	48.7	16.2
Wandsworth	1.04855	27.5	34.9	36.4
Westminster	1.2048	24.1	40.5	31.2

Significant changes were made in the AEN formula in April 1994. These included a reduction in the AEN weighting given to pupils in households where the head was born outside the UK and a reduction in the proportion of the total budget allocated by AEN, down to 17 per cent of the total. These changes had a particularly marked effect in inner London and in some metropolitan districts with high proportions of pupils from ethnic minorities, as Table 4.2 shows.

TABLE 4.2: **Selected LEAs that lose under 1994/5 AEN formula**

LEA	% Loss of education SSA 1993/4 to 1994/5	1993/4 Secondary SSA £/pupil	1994/5 Secondary SSA £/pupil	Loss in £/pupil
Lambeth	7.59	4,497	4,052	445
Hackney	6.36	4,558	4,180	378
Wandsworth	6.34	3,892	3,572	320
Westminster	6.14	3,991	3,677	314
Ealing	4.02	3,488	3,301	187
Birmingham	2.19	3,101	2,934	167
Bradford	2.13	2,940	2,791	149

The very sharp losses shown in Table 4.2 are not matched by equivalent gains in other LEAs, though there are some gainers in outer London and some of the shire counties. Some areas in the north east and north west also gained. It could be that some of these changes redress some of the effects of the previous formula. They might even represent a 'fairer' allocation, but the overall conclusion has to be that altering the formula in this way appears to have an arbitrary and sometimes dramatic effect on local authorities' capacities to support schools. Table 4.2 also shows the very wide variation in SSAs per pupil at secondary level, which range from £2,791 per pupil in Bradford to £4,180 per pupil in Hackney in 1994/95.

Allocation of central government funds based on AEN significantly affects local authority levels of expenditure on education, and, by extension, some of the striking differences in pupil-teacher ratios. The AEN formula does take some account of social needs, but has been subject to frequent change for no clear educational reasons. The overall result is SSAs which produce different levels of expenditure between LEAs that are hard to understand or justify and, worse, which tend to fluctuate sharply from year to year.

LOCAL AUTHORITY ALLOCATION TO SCHOOLS

Prior to local management of schools (LMS), the extent of financial delegation for most schools was the so-called 'capitation' allowance, something under 5 per cent of the total school budget. Under LMS the situation has altered dramatically. Apart from a few mandatory and discretionary exemptions, almost all the LEA's budget for schools (approximately 83 per cent in 1993/94) is available for delegation to schools. The legislation places an obligation on LEAs to delegate most of this so-called Potential Schools Budget (PSB). In 1990, when LMS came into effect, 85 per cent of the PSB had to be delegated; by 1993/94 the figure had risen to 90 per cent .

The amount delegated (known as the Aggregate Schools Budget or ASB) is calculated in accordance with a formula which must be approved by the Department for Education. At least 80 per cent of this must be allocated to schools in a way which relates to the numbers and ages of the pupils.

The principle of formula funding is that 'schools should be funded in strict relation to their objective need to spend rather than on their historical level of funding'. The assumption is that such formula funding is a more effective way of relating resources to needs.[14]

However, the allocation per pupil varies markedly from LEA to LEA and almost certainly reflects history rather than current need. Thus a nine year old is 'worth' £954 to a primary school in Trafford, but £1,119 to a similar school in Bolton; £944 in Wakefield, but £1,161 in Bradford. And there are also differences within the same area between pupils of different ages. Thus a ten-year-old in Salford nets £977, an 11 year old £1,593. So far the focus has been on the disparity in funding between primary and secondary schools,[15] where the average LEA spends for each primary pupil about 64 per cent of the amount allocated for a secondary pupil up to age 16.[16] But the comparison with the post-compulsory period is equally striking. Here the average LEA spends more than twice as much as per primary age pupil, and at the extremes much more. Thus, in St Helens a nine year old brings in £933 and a 16 year old £2,700. These gradients will certainly benefit schools within an LEA with high staying-on rates and large sixth forms. Secondary schools with small sixth forms or 11-16 schools will not be able to draw on this resource.

ALLOCATION FOR SOCIAL AND EDUCATIONAL NEED

The remaining 20 per cent of the allocation formula covers aspects such as support for small schools, premises and special needs. Measures of social disadvantage and non-statemented special needs have served as the basis on which many LEAs calculate additional funds for schools under this heading. Measures of children entitled to free school meals, entitlement to clothing grants and low scores on assessment tests are used by LEAs in constructing the special needs element in the funding formula. Such diversity extends from LEAs which use flat-rate entitlements (a fixed allocation per free meal or clothing grant or a system of 'banding' based on differing percentages of pupils on free school meals), to authorities which calculate 'indices' of disadvantage based on different measures.

Such diversity of criteria raises questions about the most appropriate way of assessing the additional needs of schools in disadvantaged areas. However, much more important is the amount of funding allocated to schools under this heading. CIPFA estimates for 1993/94 indicate a total of £298m allocated to schools under 'special needs'. This is just 2.6 per cent of the total schools' ASB for England and Wales. Some of the 'social needs' allocation may be recorded under the 'other expenditure' category, a further 5.4 per cent of the ASB. However, it is still less than the total allocated to 'premises' (for example, schools with split sites). And this total is, of course, the sum differentially allocated to schools on the basis of special needs, not the total available to disadvantaged schools.

Indicators of need used in formulae by different LEAs[17]

A survey conducted in July 1991 showed that of the 48 LEAs examined in England and Wales:

- 79 per cent of schemes include free school meal numbers as an indicator of need;
- 30 per cent use educational test scores;
- 19 per cent include a measure of English as a second language, ethnicity or early stages of learning English;
- 13 per cent use entitlements to clothing grants;
- 5 LEAs use the formula to fund statemented pupils;
- 4 LEAs use the formula to fund special units;
- 4 LEAs use general population data for indices of need;
- 3 LEAs base their allocation on professional assessment.

The key result is that under LMS there is very little variation in the overall budget of schools on the basis of social disadvantage – figures for individual schools suggest that overall schools in the most disadvantaged areas receive perhaps 5 per cent more funding per pupil than the bulk of schools in similar types of LEA.

There are some significant variations between LEAs. Table 4.3 shows the differences between the social needs allocation in seven LEAs, and for comparison their AEN index score.

What is also very striking is the disjunction between the allocation from central government to local authorities, particularly the AEN formula, and the subsequent allocation to schools under the LMS scheme. Of course, a certain proportion of the funds held back by the LEA go to services such as educational welfare, psychological support services and special needs units, which cater for those with social and educational needs. However, even if these are taken into account, the amount allocated to schools still may not reflect the central government allocation to the LEA.

TABLE 4.3: **The differences between the percentage of ASB allocation for special needs spending in seven LEAs compared with the SSA index score for that authority**

	% of ASB for special needs (1991)	SSA index score for AEN (1991)
Durham	0.13	0.50705
Northamptonshire	0.96	0.41385
Nottinghamshire	3.62	0.57140
Lancashire	5.86	0.54475
Leeds	8.35	0.60540
Liverpool	10.00	0.96845
North Tyneside	12.19	0.56340

Source: Lee (1991) *Additional Education Needs and LMS: methods and money 1991-2*

This disparity is shown most starkly when the Education Committee of the House of Commons demonstrated, for illustrative purposes, what would happen if the allocation criteria currently used in the SSA and AEN were applied at the school level for per pupil funding.[18] Table 4.4 shows the result for an 11-15 year old.

TABLE 4.4: **Funding per pupil if SSA allocations to LEAs were devolved to schools**

Basic amount for pupil aged 11-15	£2,096 pa
Additional if from lone parent family	£958
Additional if parent(s) on income support	£960
Additional if parent(s) from New Commonwealth	£465
Additional for each child receiving a free school meal	£50
Additional if school in sparsely populated area	(£43 average)
Additional if school in London/South East	(£109 average)

As the Committee notes, a pupil who falls into the first three categories would bring in £4,479 to the school. If this became the basis of allocation the effects on school budgets would be dramatic. Schools serving disadvantaged populations would receive an enormous boost to their funding. The present disparities of funding *between* LEAs would be transferred to schools within the same LEAs, where these differed sharply in terms of social and educational disadvantage.

Financial devolution to schools under LMS has generally been welcomed by schools. However, its introduction was combined with pressure on LEAs to devolve more to schools each year and cut back on activities under direct LEA control. Thus many schools gained in immediate cash terms. Once this source of additional funding is worked out, then the negative consequences of LMS may become more apparent. One striking finding is the very limited additions made by most LEAs for social needs. At the same time, the LEAs' discretionary powers to assist individual schools in difficulties – probably the mechanism widely used prior to LMS – have been critically weakened. Such schools are now much more on their own. Ironically, they do not benefit to the degree that they should from central government's own allocation for 'additional educational needs'. One unforeseen consequence of LMS has been the tendency for schools to build up cash balances to cushion themselves against further cuts or other uncertainties. While entirely understandable as prudent budgeting at school level, the total sum held in such school balances, now estimated to be £500m or more, can easily be used to argue that schools do not need any additional funds.

A WINDFALL FOR GRANT MAINTAINED SCHOOLS

Some schools that opted out of LEA control in the early stages under the 1988 Education Reform Act into grant maintained (GM) or 'self governing' status received a funding bonus as a result of the way LMS operates. We have already seen that many such schools received priority for capital funding projects. They also receive an annual maintenance grant (AMG) equivalent to the amount that they would have received from their local authority under LMS and a grant to cover the amount held back by the local authority for centrally run services. As local authorities were initially required to devolve 85 per cent of the PSB, this was originally set at a matching 15 per cent. But in cases where local authorities devolved more than 85 per cent to schools, the addition still remained 15 per cent, thereby providing these GM schools with an element of double funding. More than 80 per cent of GM schools in a recent survey stated that they had gained financially by opting out, and this was the second most important reason for their decision.[19]

In perspective....

...the most academically successful secondary schools in the private sector in Greater London, as identified in the *Financial Times*, have average annual fees for day pupils of £5,079 with the highest at £10,515. Compared to this, the cost per pupil of £2,000-£3,000 for educating children in the most deprived districts of inner London seems rather modest.

Times Educational Supplement, 8 April 1994

OTHER SOURCES OF FUNDING FOR SCHOOLS

GRANT FOR EDUCATION SUPPORT AND TRAINING (GEST)

Grants under the GEST programme amounted to £315m. These are direct funds to LEAs from the DFE for specific projects. A limited proportion of GEST funds have related to social disadvantage, for example, for under-fives or youth work provision, but the major amount has been linked to the national curriculum. Though initiatives under this heading have often received significant publicity, they represent quite small additions to the overall expenditure. They are also short term.

SECTION 11 FUNDING

Funds under this heading provide a very important source of additional funds to LEAs with significant ethnic minority populations. Funds have to be spent on additional teachers for English as a second language, for example, and not simply be added to the total budget. Funds under this programme totalled £144m in 1993/94 and were concentrated in particular areas. Thus, Tower Hamlets received £12m in Section 11 funding in 1993/94, approximately 10 per cent of its General Schools Budget; Birmingham and Bradford received £7m each. However, this scheme is being substantially cut back in 1994/95 and absorbed into the new 'Single Regeneration Budget'. There are fears that this will bring to an end a number of direct services for ethnic minority pupils in some of the most disadvantaged urban areas. The Urban Programme, which like Section 11 also dated from the 1960s, and at its peak significantly added to educational expenditure, has already been largely phased out. Only £2m in total was received by LEAs under this programme in 1993/94.

FUNDS RAISED BY SCHOOLS

Schools have always raised funds independently. But what is new is the extent to which schools in the maintained sector are increasingly relying on such funding. There is evidence that this is increasing, becoming more uneven between schools of different types and more frequently used to support essential components of the school's programme. These developments are clearly linked to the changing methods of funding schools and stem directly from the idea of schools as 'independent enterprises' making their own way and competing for resources. While it would be difficult to argue against schools or their Parent-Teacher Associations (PTAs) taking the initiative to raise funds, legitimate concerns arise where this results in significant inequalities between schools and where it becomes increasingly necessary in order to compensate for reduced levels of LEA funding.

It is also important to identify the different sources of additional income. This may come from parents or local people, from industry or commerce, from charitable funds or sometimes, importantly, from the sub-letting of premises. While some of these sources may depend on school or parent initiative, significant sub-letting may depend either on having attractive and well-located premises, or on having surplus space which can be permanently sub-let.

In 1990 the National Confederation of Parent Teacher Associations (NCPTA) surveyed its home school associations.[20] The results showed a rise in funds raised from an average of £5.71 per pupil at primary level in 1985 to £8.53 in 1990; and at secondary school from £2.77 to £4.81 over the same period. These increases were significantly above the rate of inflation. Judged against the LEA average capitation figure for 1989/90, this represented 27 per cent of capitation at primary schools and 7 per cent at secondary. Over the same period increasing proportions of these funds were for essential items in the school's budget.[21] Grossed up for schools in general these figures suggested that some £55m was being contributed annually by home-school associations.

In a survey of a sample of 445 primary schools in 1990, Sumner and Hutchinson from the National Foundation for Educational Research in England and Wales (NFER)[22] provide more extensive information about funds raised by primary schools from sources other than LEA capitation (not just from PTAs). They found that an average sum of £13 per pupil was raised with very wide and significant variations. Thus 28 of the schools raised less than £1 per pupil but one raised more than £100 per pupil. Overall the sum raised was just over half the sum provided in capitation by the LEA (51.5 per cent). There were regional variations, with schools in the south raising an average £14.41; those in Wales £8.29. Those in the inner city raised £7.43; those in county towns/rural areas £18.84 – more than twice as much per pupil. Sumner and Hutchinson found that almost 80 per cent of schools in their study 'were spending funds raised by parents on essentials for learning'.[23]

Bullock and Thomas show a very similar picture in their LMS study. Seventy-nine per cent of schools supplemented their budgets by fundraising, with considerable variations in the amounts raised. The clear message from several comments was that such fundraising 'used to be used for extras, but now money raised goes into the "big pot"'.[24] While there are some exceptions where schools have raised significant amounts, figures from HMI suggest that the average was about 1 per cent of the total budget.

However, recent data from GM schools suggest that some of these schools may be raising very large sums through specialist fundraising as well as sub-letting of premises. One school quotes a figure of £700,000 raised through a variety of mechanisms.[25]

SUMMARY AND CONCLUSION: INEQUALITIES OF FUNDING

- Overall spending on schools has not kept pace with growth in the economy over the last 20 years. Overall expenditure has risen only marginally since 1975.
- Funding per pupil has risen, but largely as the result of a steep decline in pupil numbers during the 1980s. LEAs successfully maintained educational spending despite pressure from central government. The introduction of very tight capping on local authority expenditure and now rising numbers at primary level, plus the surge in post-16 numbers, has meant falling per pupil expenditure in recent years, particularly at secondary level.
- Capital expenditure has fallen and remained very low since the late 1970s. Expenditure on maintenance is now at a level significantly below that required, with a growing backlog.

- Central government allocation to local authorities for education has since 1990 had a significantly raised level of allocation based on the AEN formula. However, while generally tipped towards more disadvantaged areas, this allocation has revealed a number of serious anomalies with higher allocations going to some local authorities with objectively lower levels of need than other areas.
- Changes in the AEN allocations in April 1994 have meant a substantial loss of funding for LEAs with significant ethnic minority populations.
- Differences in the LMS formula mean some very large discrepancies both within the same LEA for different age groups and between apparently similar schools in apparently similar LEAs.
- Under LMS, LEAs are entitled to include an element for social disadvantage/special need. However, the picture is one of great variability. Up to 12 per cent of ASB may be allocated according to criteria of social need by some LEAs and much less than 1 per cent in others.
- Social disadvantage, special educational needs and the needs of ethnic minorities tend to be rolled together with a range of different criteria by different LEAs. The same LEA may change the formula and there is no evidence of a standard pattern.
- The total amount of funds allocated to schools on social needs grounds is very small. In many LEAs there is therefore very little variation in school budgets for advantaged or disadvantaged areas.
- There is virtually no linkage between the AEN allocation to local authorities and the elements in their LMS allocation to schools in either method or amount. Such linkage would have a dramatic impact on the budgets of schools serving disadvantaged areas.
- A substantial proportion of schools, particularly those with falling rolls and high staffing or fixed costs, or which received substantial help from the LEA in the past, are likely to be 'losers' under the LMS allocation policy because of the fixed formula, even though they may receive transitional protection in the short term. Such schools face a steady reduction in their funding.
- Although the introduction of LMS formulae introduces a clear element of 'formal rationality', it virtually eradicates local authorities' capacity to act flexibly in response to changing needs.
- For many disadvantaged schools and areas, funding from programmes such as the Home Office Section 11 and the DoE Urban Programme has resulted in significant extra resources, to a degree differentially allocated according to social need. Both these funding

programmes have now been cut or phased out.

- As schools have moved towards greater financial autonomy, school-based fundraising has taken on much greater significance. There are high levels of variation by area. This also applies to funds raised from other sources, such as from sub-letting, local industry or even from charity. These funds are increasingly being used to support essential school activities, rather than as extras.

Part of the Government's philosophy behind current educational reforms is to create greater autonomy for individual schools to pursue their own path, thereby creating much greater diversity. What is clear from the evidence on funding allocation is that this philosophy carries the strong possibility of increasing inequalities. What is striking is the very large number of anomalies in the present system, which are hard to understand and even harder to justify. Recent changes will almost certainly increase this diversity, with some schools having increasingly greater command over resources, while others decline.

NOTES

1. Quoted in National Association of Head Teachers, *Resources in Education 1993-4*, 1993.
2. Education Committee of the House of Commons, *The Disparity in Funding between Primary and Secondary Schools*, HMSO, 13 July 1994, Appendix 21.
3. See, for example, reports from the Education Committee of the House of Commons during 1994.
4. Department for Education, *Statistical Bulletin 4/94 Education Expenditure from 1979-80*, 1994, Table 7.
5. Department of Education and Science, *UK Statistics of Education*, 1991 edition, Tables 5 and 6 (data for the UK).
6. Chartered Institute of Public Finance Accountants (CIPFA), *Education Statistics 1992-93 Actuals*, October 1994, Table 5.
7. Senior Chief Inspector, *Standards of Education 1989-90*, the Annual Report of HM Senior Chief Inspector of Schools, 1991.
8. Organisation for Economic Co-operation and Development (OECD), *Education at a Glance*, 1993, Table P5.
9. National Audit Office, *Repair and Maintenance of School Buildings*, HMSO, 1991.
10. *Ibid*, p16.
11. Fourth Report of the Select Committee, *The DFE's Expenditure Plans 1993-4 to 1995-6*, HMSO, 27 October 1993, para 77.
12. *Times Educational Supplement*, 12 August 1994.

13. Independent Schools Information Service (ISIS), *Annual Census 1994*, April 1994.
14. T Lee, *Carving Out Cash for Schools: LMS and the new ERA of education*, Centre for the Analysis of Social Policy, University of Bath, 1990.
15. Education Committee of the House of Commons, *op cit.*
16. *Ibid*, J Hardman and R Levacic, Appendix 20.
17. T Lee, *Additional Education Needs and LMS: methods and money 1991-2*, Centre for the Analysis of Social Policy, University of Bath, 1992.
18. Education Committee of the House of Commons, *A Common Funding Formula for Grant Maintained Schools*, HMSO, April 1994, pxii.
19. *Times Educational Supplement*, 7 October 1994.
20. National Confederation of Parent Teacher Associations (NCPTA), *The State of Schools in England and Wales*, November 1991.
21. *Ibid*, Table 3, p18.
22. R Sumner and D Hutchinson, *Resources in Primary Schools*, NFER, 1990.
23. *Ibid*, p19.
24. A Bullock and H Thomas, *The Impact of Local Management of Schools*, University of Birmingham, 1994, p20.
25. *Times Educational Supplement*, 7 October 1994.

5 Access and choice: from parents to 'consumers'

Pupils are to be educated in accordance with the wishes of their parents.

1944 Education Act

You have a duty to ensure that your child gets an education – and you can choose the school that you would like your child to go to. Your choice is wider as a result of recent changes... You have a right to say which school you prefer... You have a right to a place in the school you want unless it is full to capacity with pupils who have a stronger claim.

Parent's Charter, 1991

The implementation of market reforms in education is essentially a class strategy which has as one of its major effects the reproduction of relative social class (and ethnic) advantages and disadvantages.

Ball, 1993

Choice is not a new principle in education. But the aim of making parental choice the driving force in education moves way beyond anything envisaged by the 1944 Education Act, which was intended to satisfy religious preferences rather than ensure individual choice of school. The idea is that of a market, where parents act as consumers making choices on behalf of their children, from a range of educational services. Nobody would argue against greater choice, in principle. But the question is how choice works in practice. In the previous chapter we looked at educational funding, and spelt out some of the growing inequalities and anomalies affecting different schools and areas. Here we ask a similar question. Does the market ensure equal access to all, or does it strengthen existing advantages and disadvantages?

In this chapter we consider the impact of the new policies designed to increase choice for parents, particularly on families in disadvantaged areas. These policies include 'the right to choose', 'open enrolment' and special schemes such as the Assisted Places Scheme; new types of school such as the City Technology Colleges; and 'diversity' within the state system through 'opted out' schools and 'specialisation'. We also look at the growing problem of exclusions.

NEW POLICIES: 'THE RIGHT TO CHOOSE' AND 'OPEN ENROLMENT'

The 1980 Education Act foreshadowed the legislation on parental choice to come in the late 1980s and early 1990s when it established rights for parents to sit on governing bodies and 'to express a preference' for an individual school, and required governors to provide information for parents on criteria for admission, examination results, and curriculum. Yet the effects were very variable, with some authorities encouraging choice and others attempting to restrict it on the grounds that long-term planning was essential for efficiency. Local education authorities could still set an admissions limit below a school's 'standard number'.

The 1988 Education Reform Act abolished this power (schools could take pupils up to and, if they wished, above the 'standard number') and introduced 'open enrolment' – that is, parents' right not merely to 'express a preference' but to place their children in the school of their choice. And according to the Parent's Charter, parents now have an even wider choice, since 'open enrolment' applies across local education authority boundaries: the 'Greenwich' judgment made it illegal for admission authorities to favour applicants on the basis of the authority in which they lived – that is, to discriminate between 'in-borough' and 'out-borough' pupils.

Parents can in theory choose their children's school – provided the school has a place. If the school is full, the child will be offered a place elsewhere. Popular schools, of course, are likely to be full and under great pressure both from prospective parents to expand and from existing parents to limit their size. In this situation, we might expect schools to choose their parents rather than parents to choose their children's schools. What evidence is there that 'parents as consumers' *do* have equal access in the market to the schools of their choice? And what criteria do parents employ in making their choices?

There is as yet insufficient evidence to answer these questions in

England. But 'open enrolment' has been in operation in Scotland for longer and the findings of research there may be taken as a good indication of the likely effects of the 1988 Education Reform Act. What is clear from the Scottish studies[1] is that choice, operating largely, though not entirely, along social class lines, has the effect of reinforcing already existing social and educational divisions.

But first, let us put this issue into perspective. Parents choosing to appeal against their child's school place are in a minority. This is confirmed by the experience of local education authorities south of the border which claim that approximately 90 per cent of parents got their first choice of school *before* the new legislation came into effect.[2] Figures for Scotland show that 15 per cent of pupils in the first year of primary school and 11.5 per cent in the first year of secondary school were the subject of a 'placing request' (that is, an appeal against the designated school).[3]

Appeals are not randomly distributed; rates are substantially higher in urban areas, where there are more schools within easy reach, than in rural areas, where transport costs may preclude choice. It is also clear that many parents make their choices on inadequate information – often limited, second-hand and out-of-date.

It is not only middle class parents who exercise their right to choose a school other than that designated for their child. But working class and middle class parents may make their choices on different grounds. In some of the Scottish studies, working class parents in disadvantaged areas were choosing to avoid the local neighbourhood school in favour of schools in more middle class or socially mixed areas, while few middle class parents chose to send their children to school in a disadvantaged estate. Choice may operate differently for middle class and working class parents in other ways. There is some evidence that the latter value the proximity, local and community aspects of a school in their own right.[4] The atmosphere and ethos of a school, and whether the child's friends have chosen to go there, may be judged as important as academic success.

Other studies show that parents making a choice were more highly educated themselves and had more prestigious jobs than those accepting their children's designated school. They tended to choose the more academic schools catering for a more middle class clientele. These parents' choices may be rational ones – if they increase their own children's chances of success. But the overall effect of individual choice has been to increase both educational inequalities between schools and social polarisation, as schools serving disadvantaged areas lost pupils and consequently finance and teachers. Thus choice has high costs for the education system as a whole. This may be particularly the case if parents are choosing on 'negative' grounds – trying to avoid the local neighbourhood school – rather than making an 'optimal' choice from a wide range of possible schools.

Choice requires knowledge of local schools, ability to find out information, understanding of often complicated admissions procedures, engagement with schools' promotional events like open evenings, and the capacity to present a 'good image' as well as operate the appeals procedure. We find similar examples elsewhere: in one study in Chicago, parents exercising their right to choose were typically middle class – 'well connected to networks of information and influence', and energetic in 'mastering the intricacies of admissions and negotiating the outcomes they wanted'.[5] Inability, unwillingness or ignorance of 'the system' on the part of less educated or less confident parents may lead to 'self-exclusion' – based perhaps on a belief that the system does not work for them.

The idea of 'parents as consumers' assumes that parents will make different but equally effective choices about the best and most suitable education for their children, and that they start from the same point in making those choices. However, it is abundantly clear that 'choice' operates differently for different groups. The Scottish studies concluded that parental choice poses a serious challenge to equality of educational opportunity and has led to the re-emergence of a two-tier system, with a minority of 'rump' schools catering for the most disadvantaged areas of the big cities.[6]

NEW POLICIES: 'OPTING OUT'

The grant maintained (GM) schools policy, which encouraged schools to leave local education authority control and become self-governing, was announced in the Conservative manifesto for the 1987 general election and was incorporated into the Educational Reform Act 1988. The policy was represented as a means of extending parental choice, improving standards and diversifying provision – an opportunity to 'take education out of the hands of planners and return it to parents where it belongs'.[7] But the crucial question is whether grant maintained schools can be said to increase choice for *all*, or only for *some*.

Opting out is a divisive move, if we consider the relationship between the school and its neighbourhood. By withdrawing a school lost pupils and consequently finance and teachers. Thus choic high costs for the education system as a whole. This may be partic the case if parents are choosing on 'negative' grounds – tryi avoid the local neighbourhood school – rather than making an 'op choice from a wide range of possible schools.

Choice requires knowledge of local schools, ability to finc information, understanding of often complicated admis procedures, engagement with schools' promotional events like evenings, and the capacity to present a 'good image' as well as op the appeals procedure. We find similar examples elsewhere: in study in Chicago, parents exercising their right to choose were typ middle class – 'well connected to networks of information influence', and energetic in 'mastering the intricacies of admis and negotiating the outcomes they wanted'.[5] Inability, unwillin or ignorance of 'the system' on the part of less educated or confident parents may lead to 'self-exclusion' – based perhaps belief that the system does not work for them.

The idea of 'parents as consumers' assumes that parents will different but equally effective choices about the best and most sui education for their children, and that they start from the same in making those choices. However, it is abundantly clear that 'ch operates differently for different groups. The Scottish studies concl that parental choice poses a serious challenge to equality of educati opportunity and has led to the re-emergence of a two-tier sys with a minority of 'rump' schools catering for the most disadvant areas of the big cities.[6]

NEW POLICIES: 'OPTING OUT'

The grant maintained (GM) schools policy, which encouraged sch to leave local education authority control and become self-govern was announced in the Conservative manifesto for the 1987 gen election and was incorporated into the Educational Reform Act 19 The policy was represented as a means of extending parental cho improving standards and diversifying provision – an opportunity 'take education out of the hands of planners and return it to pare where it belongs'.[7] But the crucial question is whether grant maintai schools can be said to increase choice for *all*, or only for *some*.

Opting out is a divisive move, if we consider the relations between the school and its neighbourhood. By withdrawing a sch compared with the 4 per cent of selective secondary schools in the LEA sector before the grant maintained policy took effect. Selection might, of course, be done informally on social, economic or other criteria, through pupil/parental interviews, rather than on formal academic criteria such as testing or primary school reports. The first wave of opting out also included a high number of single sex schools.

In a recent survey by the *Times Educational Supplement* some 10 per cent of the GM schools surveyed were planning to change they way they selected pupils.[12]

Specialisation, choice or discrimination?

- A newly 'opted out' comprehensive school proposed to end a long-standing scheme to integrate blind and partially sighted pupils from the special school on the other side of the shared playing field unless additional funds were found for support staff and equipment.
  Guardian, 17 August 1993
- The Commission for Racial Equality found two grant-maintained schools, both heavily over-subscribed, guilty of discriminating against Asian applicants, who were half as likely to get places as non-Asian applicants. However, the schools concerned were following their previous LEA's admissions procedures – which means that discrimination was not limited to 'opted-out' schools.
  Times Educational Supplement, 31 January 1992
- Grammar schools and comprehensives with academic streams in Essex are to run a series of tests for up to 7,000 pupils on a Saturday in the New Year. Four schools in Hertfordshire will be selecting half their intake on the basis of aptitude tests from next autumn. And an 850-pupil school in Grantham is to move to entry by 11-plus achievement only. Other secondary heads are looking to select pupils on the basis of talent in the arts or technology.
  Times Educational Supplement, 7 October 1994

So far, it is clear that the new policy has not provided much in the way of new opportunities for children in poorer families, or an extension of choice for their parents. Fitz, Power and Halpin[13] showed that only a few grant maintained schools in their survey served areas that could be defined as disadvantaged – only 8 per cent of the 225 schools in the 55 LEAs surveyed where schools were opting out.

But it is also clear that although only a minority of schools have so far taken this route, even one school in an authority choosing to do so may have a considerable impact on the overall provision and planning of services, and the financing of other schools. Typical reasons for 'opting out' are schools seeking grant maintained status when they feel threatened by amalgamation or closure, or by LEA proposals for restructuring.[14] A handful of authorities now have very high concentrations of grant maintained schools, where secondary education may be moving out of local authority control altogether. By late 1994, this is the case for Hillingdon, with control of secondary education passing to the Funding Agency for Schools.[15]

Overall, the evidence suggests that 'privileging piecemeal, individual rationality in the way envisaged by the grant-maintained schools policy strengthens, rather than ameliorates, basic inequalities within the education service as a whole'.[16] The conclusion so far is that the grant maintained policy is likely to hinder the introduction of egalitarian measures by LEA's aimed at benefiting disadvantaged children, and in some cases to lead to a two-tier system reinforcing present social inequalities.

THE ASSISTED PLACES SCHEME

The Assisted Places Scheme (APS) formed part of the 1980 Education Act and met the Conservative pledge to restore 'the direct-grant principle' to enable 'bright children from modest backgrounds' 'who might not otherwise be able to do so to benefit from education at independent schools'. Financial assistance was to be provided for tuition fees, on a sliding scale linked to parental income, with provision for expenses such as uniforms, travel, school meals, etc. Although it has been subsequently defined as the first step in the Conservative Government's agenda for privatising the education system,[17] at the time Mark Carlisle, the Minister responsible for implementing the scheme, set it firmly within the tradition of the 'scholarship ladder' and parental choice:

> I didn't look upon it as a privatisation measure at all ... I did promote it on two points – the basic scholarship idea and secondly as a general widening of choice for parents.[18]

Statistics showing that over 40 per cent of 'assisted places' parents were eligible for full fee remission and that a further 11 per cent paid

£100 or less in fees per annum have been used as evidence that the scheme has been effective in achieving its goals. However, it has been argued that the scheme 'has not in practice yet opened up real opportunities for that very group which according to the scheme's original rhetoric of legitimisation, would otherwise be trapped in poor neighbourhood comprehensives in the inner city'.[19] Survey findings show that the scheme has in fact benefited a particular group of individuals who had 'the educational and cultural capacity necessary to unlock the gate to an assisted passage through the fee-paying independent schools' and whose cultural and political resources would have enabled them to 'escape' within the state sector anyway.[20]

An analysis of the take-up of places is an obvious check on whether the scheme has been successful when judged on its own terms. What is the evidence that assisted places are reaching the target group – 'bright children from modest backgrounds'?

There have been a number of studies of the scheme.[21] The original image of the 'ideal client' was that of 'an able boy or girl from a working class inner city home being "rescued" from the academic inadequacies of local comprehensive schools' – while critics of the scheme 'were convinced that such pupils would not figure extensively among its beneficiaries'.[22] One study compared the social and educational backgrounds of assisted-place pupils with those of contemporaries paying full fees in the same schools, and of pupils of the same age attending maintained schools in the state sector. This showed that very few children of working class parents had taken up assisted places. Less than 10 per cent of children taking up assisted places had fathers in manual work, compared with 50 per cent whose fathers were professionals, managers or high or medium grade workers in service industries. Although this study was looking at data in the 1980s, what it found has been likened to the composition of direct grant schools in the 1960s when approximately 60 per cent of their intake came from professional/managerial families compared with some 8 per cent from the manual working class. Assisted place pupils and full fee payers both tended to be children from professional and middle-class families – *not* from the working classes.

However, it was clear that a high proportion of assisted place pupils came from low-income families. This has been partly explained by the large numbers of children of professional parents on average national income – clergyman and teachers in particular. But the main explanation lies in the fact that 40 per cent of the assisted place families were headed by lone parents. This marked over-representation has been widely claimed to indicate the scheme's success in matching opportunity with need. However, it is significant that children from other types of family often defined as disadvantaged (unemployed, semi-skilled or unskilled, black and Asian) were conspicuously absent from the scheme. But lone parent families are diverse in status and circumstances. The scheme considers income, not wealth, and only *parental* income, in determining eligibility. Lone parent status often came together with a social background of considerable educational advantage – what might be called 'educational inheritance'. Sixty-eight per cent of the mothers and 51 per cent of the fathers of assisted place pupils had themselves been to either private or selective schools; levels of educational qualification were high compared with national averages. 'Relevant income' may not be a reliable guide to the cultural and educational situations of families.

Another study[23] concludes that 'relatively few Assisted Place Scheme students come from unambiguously working-class backgrounds: substantial numbers of Assisted Place Scheme students come from one-parent families or from homes where the low income level reflects "unusual" circumstances such as unemployment, rather than the normal occupation of the main wage earner; many Assisted Place Scheme students are drawn from within the "independent school frame of reference" in the sense that relatives had attended or worked at such a school, or that they would have attended independent schools anyway'.

It has also been argued that the scheme has provided a significant subsidy to private schools from the state.[24] The scheme has been described as a 'scholarship ladder' premised on selective secondary education which benefits the 'artificially poor'. Location, neighbourhood catchment policies and a deficit in 'cultural capital' may all have prevented children from disadvantaged backgrounds from benefiting.

A NEW TYPE OF SCHOOL: CITY TECHNOLOGY COLLEGES

First announced in October 1986, there were 15 City Technology Colleges (CTCs) by September 1993. Statistically insignificant, as they will educate less than 1 per cent of the secondary school population, they are nonetheless important as 'the first radically new type of school to be created since the 1944 Act'.[25] The aim was to extend choice and diversity, and raise standards in the inner cities, as set out in the Department of Education and Science booklet, *City Technology Colleges: a new choice of school*:

> The Government believes that this aim [to improve standards] will be achieved more quickly and more effectively if parents have a greater say in, and can feel more responsible for, their children's education ... There are many examples of good schooling offered by committed teachers in the cities. But many families living there who seek the best possible education for their children do not have access to the kind of schools which measure up to their ambitions...[26]

Early proposals met with considerable opposition from industry and business and from local education authorities, which in many cases felt that existing schools were being threatened, and long-standing links with schools and neighbourhoods, which had taken many years to build up, ignored: 'an entirely new school on your patch ... will probably recruit some of your best teachers and cream off some of your pupils'.[27]

To what extent have CTCs benefited poor children in urban areas? Although CTCs' intakes were intended to be broadly 'representative' of their neighbourhood, rather than academically selective, they could select students on a broad range of much less easily defined or measured criteria, including parents' and children's motivation and commitment to the school. It is clear that CTCs look for children and families with particular interests or abilities, and may well select those who already have a high interest in education: to this extent, CTCs may well be said to 'sponsor' some of the 'deserving poor' out of their environment.[28] However, while individual CTCs claim significant numbers from working class and ethnic minority groups, it is not clear how representative these are of their local neighbourhoods. One study concluded that 'families not already valuing education are less likely to apply and, if they do apply, less likely to be able to convince the CTCs that they should be selected. Those children most in need will not benefit from the CTCs.'[29]

ADMISSIONS POLICY BY DEFAULT? – EXCLUSIONS FROM SCHOOL

Although schools moving formally to specialisation or a selective admissions policy are still in a minority, the enormous rise in exclusions creates what in effect is for some pupils a *de facto* admissions policy.

With schools managing their own finances (LMS), there is now 'every incentive to schools to exclude "problems" rather than to respond to them'.[30] This is particularly the case for hard-pressed schools serving hard-pressed areas and particular groups are most at risk – adolescents labelled disruptive and Afro-Caribbean youngsters.

Dumping the disaffected

'Parents and professionals fear the market underpinning the education system, with schools competing through league tables and glossy brochures, is leading to widespread exclusion of pupils for more trivial offences. Worries that children thought to be more disaffected or difficult are losing out have been highlighted by statistics showing that particular groups, such as Afro-Caribbean boys, are likeliest to be excluded.'

Times Educational Supplement, 1 July 1994, 'Exclusions "bias" to be investigated'

The Education Act (No. 2) 1986 defined three types of exclusion from school: fixed term (formerly known as suspension), indefinite (in which a date for return is agreed after consultation) and permanent (formerly known as expulsion). (Indefinite exclusion has been abolished by the Education Act 1993 s261.[31]) There is no doubt that the number of exclusions from school is rising, particularly permanent 'expulsions'. Gloucestershire reported more permanent exclusions in the winter term 1991 than in the whole of the year 1990/91.[32] Sheffield reported a 65 per cent increase in permanent exclusions in 1990/91 compared with the previous year, and Birmingham an increase of 20 per cent over the previous three years.[33] The Advisory Centre for Education (ACE) wrote to all LEAs in 1992 asking for information on exclusions between 1986 and 1991. It found[34] that the rate of increase in the use of permanent exclusions rose from 39 per cent between September 1986 and July 1988 to 66 per cent between September 1988 and July 1991. In 21 out of 28 LEAs there had been an increase in all three categories. In others, while indefinite exclusions had fallen, fixed and permanent exclusions had risen. Other surveys suggest increases of between 20 per cent and 50 per cent in 1990–1992. A survey by the National Association for Head Teachers in the autumn term 1994 suggested growing rates of permanent exclusions in many LEAs.[35]

The ACE survey also revealed 'a whole catalogue of illegal procedures and poor practice'. For example, exclusion letters were often vague or confusing; parents often felt they or their children had been unfairly treated; some schools failed to provide excluded pupils with homework; parents were sometimes persuaded 'informally' to remove their children from school, before formal exclusion procedures were spelt out; few parents knew their rights to see their child's school record. ACE also reported a large increase in telephone calls from parents wanting advice over exclusions – from an average 6 per cent of all telephone enquiries in 1988 to 13 per cent in 1991.

Do schools exclude black children?

The Office for Standards in Education (OFSTED) reported in 1993 (*Education for Disaffected Pupils*) that in one LEA black youngsters accounted for 1:4 exclusions although they made up only 1:14 pupil population, while in another LEA the figures were 85 per cent and 17 per cent. It is probable, too, that children being looked after ('in care') feature disproportionately in those excluded.

Birmingham's lists in 1992 showed that black youngsters accounted for 32 per cent of all exclusions but made up only 8 per cent of the school population.

Times Educational Supplement, 31 July 1992

There is also little doubt that particular groups are at risk – especially adolescents labelled 'disruptive'.[36] 'Disruptive adolescents' may well leave school before exclusions are resolved, particularly if they are 'passed round' from school to school.[37] Afro-Caribbean pupils are also much more likely than white pupils to face exclusion. In its case files, the Institute of Race Relations has documented the 'culture of exclusion' – case studies which clearly illustrate the different reactions to behaviour by black and white pupils. Cultural style or religious custom may be misunderstood, medical or educational problems misdiagnosed, provocation or the racial content of incidents ignored, questions taken as accusations or threats:

> Black children (are seen as) ... particularly intractable behavioural problems by virtue of their culture, family structure or upbringing. The exclusion of the black child ... is ... regarded as another element in the social pathology of the black family...[38]

> Black children seemed to attract an inordinately harsh punishment for a misdemeanour for which white children might not be punished ... Some teachers take any querying of their decisions by black children

> as an accusation of racism; others are swift to label the individual black child as insubordinate and a group of black pupils as threatening and disruptive.[39]

The Commission for Racial Equality carried out a formal investigation in Birmingham of pupils suspended from schools between 1974 and 1980 which showed that black children were almost four times as likely to be suspended than white pupils, making up 10 per cent of the school population but 40 per cent of the exclusions. The Institute of Race Relations survey gave similar examples from Wolverhampton, Nottingham, Lewisham, Southwark and Brent.[40]

Official figures for 1990[41] show that 15 was the peak age for exclusions; boys outnumbered girls by about four to one; 12.5 per cent of excluded pupils had statements of special educational needs; and disobedience in various forms (refusal to obey school rules, verbal abuse or insolence to teachers) was the most common reason for exclusion. Suspension rates vary considerably from area to area and from school to school in a way that seems to have little to do with either the incidence of disruptive behaviour or the socio-economic nature of schools' catchment areas. In a study of one LEA,[42] schools reported that two-thirds of all exclusions over three years (1988/89-1991/92) were over issues to do with pupil management and control (45 per cent for bullying, fighting or verbally abusing other students; 22 per cent for disruption, misconduct, 'defiance', 'disobedience' and 'unacceptable behaviour'). Physical abuse or assault of staff accounted for only 1 per cent of all exclusions (although 12 per cent were for verbal abuse of staff), echoing the Elton Committee's findings in 1989.[43]

As for the *increase* in exclusions, the NUT survey of 1992 suggested that this was caused by the general lack of resources, increased competition between schools and the pressure from school testing and league tables, and poor home circumstances and lack of parental discipline.[44] OFSTED says that 'there are no clear reasons ... although some hypotheses have been proffered'.[45] It lists a number of possible reasons: increased stress in families, resulting in difficult behaviour in school; staffing difficulties in inner-city schools; a breakdown in informal arrangements between head teachers considering exclusions; and attempts to secure or maintain resources for children needing extra support. One study[46] of schools serving poor areas which have a low exclusion rate suggests that a 'child-centred' ethos of flexible discipline and allowances for students in distress is the most important aspect. But problems of family stress and lack of school resources might well apply, particularly to schools in poor areas. If this is indeed the case, then we have one more example of how access and choice may be further restricted for children of poor families.

Recent information suggests that there are now in many inner city areas significant numbers of secondary age pupils effectively excluded from schooling.[47]

SUMMARY: ACCESS AND CHOICE – 'THE RIGHT TO CHOOSE'?

We began this chapter with the claim from the Parent's Charter about 'choice' and 'access' – that parents can now choose their children's schools. Enough has been said, however, to throw considerable doubt on this claim (even in its weaker version of a 'right to state a preference'). Exclusion from school is the most worrying of all the policies discussed in this chapter, because it affects every school and all age groups. Here the rise in numbers, and the differences in exclusion policy between schools, areas and groups, bear more heavily on particular groups – and particularly schools in high stress areas with low levels of resources for pupils who need extra help.

Grant maintained schools, presented as an opportunity to 'take education out of the hands of planners and return it to parents where it belongs', are more likely to reduce than increase parental choice, by increased selectivity of intake – and are unlikely to serve poorer neighbourhoods. The Assisted Places Scheme, hailed as 'a general widening of choice for parents' and a chance for 'bright children from modest backgrounds', has, it seems, been of more benefit to children from middle class families in straitened circumstances. But, more important, it appears that 'open enrolment' and 'the right to choose' in the mainstream statutory sector do not extend choice equally to all. 'Choice', even in mainstream schooling, is shown to be paper-thin when there is pressure on popular schools – except for the most articulate and persistent parents.

NOTES

1. M Adler, A Petch and J Tweedie, *Parental Choice and Educational Policy*, Edinburgh University Press, 1989; J D Willms and F Echols, 'Alert and inert clients: the Scottish experience of parental choice of schools', *Economics of Education Review*, 11(4), 1992, pp339-50.

2. For example, Oxfordshire.
3. Scottish Education Department, *Placing Requests in Education Authority Schools*, Statistical Bulletin Edn/B6/1992/13, 1992.
4. S J Ball, S Gewirtz and R Bowe, 'Circuits of schooling: a sociological exploration of parental choice of school in social class contexts', *British Educational Research Association* conference paper, Stirling, 1992.
5. D Moore, 'Voice and choice in Chicago', in W Clune and J Witte (eds), *Choice and Control in American Education, vol 2*, Falmer Press, 1990.
6. M Adler, *An Alternative Approach to Parental Choice*, NCE Briefing No.13, National Commission on Education, 1993.
7. Centre for Policy Studies, 'Advice to the Secretary of State', in J Haviland (ed), *Take Care Mr Baker!*, Fourth Estate, 1988, p108.
8. See Chapter 4 for details of the funding of grant maintained schools.
9. Local Schools Information, *Guide to the Issue of Opting Out*, 1994, p7.
10. Figures quoted in *Times Educational Supplement*, 8 July 1994, p2.
11. J Fitz, S Power and D Halpin, 'Opting for grant maintained status: a study of policy making in education', *Policy Studies*, 14(1), pp4-20.
12. *Times Educational Supplement*, 7 October 1994.
13. Fitz, Power and Halpin, *op cit*.
14. D Halpin, S Power and J Fitz, 'Grant-maintained schools: making a difference without being different', *British Journal of Educational Studies*, 39(4), pp409-24.
15. C Dean, 'Councils map route back for GM schools', *Times Educational Supplement*, 29 July 1994.
16. Halpin, Power and Fitz, *op cit*, p414.
17. R Pring, 'Privatisation of education', *Journal of Educational Policy*, 2(4), pp289-99.
18. Quoted in J Fitz, T Edwards and G Whitty,'The Assisted Places Scheme: an ambiguous case of privatisation', *British Journal of Educational Studies*, 37(3), pp222-34.
19. T Edwards, J Fitz and G Whitty, *The State and Private Education: an evaluation of the Assisted Places Scheme*, Falmer Press, 1989.
20. *Ibid*, p215.
21. *Ibid*; M Douse, 'The background of assisted place scheme students', *Educational Studies*, 11(3), 1985, pp211-17; G Walford, 'The Scottish Assisted Places Scheme: a comparative study of the origins, nature and practice of the Assisted Places Scheme in Scotland, England and Wales', *Journal of Educational Policy*, 3(2), 1988, pp137-54.
22. Edwards, Fitz and Whitty, *op cit*.
23. Douse, *op cit*.
24. Walford, *op cit*.
25. G Walford, *Choice and Equity in Education*, Cassell, 1994, p56.
26. Department of Education and Science, *City Technology Colleges: a new choice of school*, 1986, p3.

27. Bob Finch, education liaison officer for ICI, *Times Educational Supplement*, 1 February 1991, quoted in G Whitty, T Edwards and S Gewirtz, *Specialisation and Choice in Urban Education: the City Technology College experiment*, Routledge, 1993.
28. Walford, *op cit*, p94.
29. Walford, *ibid*, p80.
30. Howard Knight, Chair of Finance, Sheffield City Council, writing in *The Guardian*, 28 January 1992, quoted in A Imich, 'Exclusions from school: current trends and issues', *Educational Research*, 36(1), 1994, p8.
31. See Department for Education, *Pupils with Problems*, Circular 10/94, *Exclusions from School*, 1994, para 8.
32. *Times Educational Supplement*, 24 April 1992.
33. *Times Educational Supplement*, 4 October 1991.
34. Advisory Centre for Education, *Findings from ACE Investigations into Exclusions. ACE advice line survey. Findings from analysis of articles of government*, mimeo; Advisory Centre for Education, *Exclusions*, Bulletin No.45, January 1992.
35. Reports by MORI and the National Union of Teachers, *Times Educational Supplement*, 2 April 1993; letter to Gillian Shephard, Secretary of State for Education, 6 December 1994.
36. *Times Educational Supplement*, 17 July 1992; Department for Education, *Pupils with Problems*.
37. See, for example, *Times Educational Supplement*, 17 July 1992.
38. J Bourne, L Bridges and C Searle, *Outcast England: how schools exclude black children*, Institute of Race Relations, 1994, pv.
39. *Ibid*, pp34-5.
40. Quoted in *ibid*, pp41-2.
41. Figures from the National Exclusions Reporting Systems (NERS) reported in Department for Education, *Exclusions – a discussion paper*, DFE, 1992.
42. A Imich, 'Exclusions from school: current trends and issues', *Educational Research*, 36(1), 1994, pp3-11.
43. Department of Education and Science, *Discipline in Schools*, the Elton Report, HMSO, 1989.
44. National Union of Teachers, *NUT Survey on Pupils' Exclusions: information from LEAs*, NUT report, June 1992.
45. Office for Standards in Education, *Education for Disaffected Pupils*, OFSTED, 1993, para 11.
46. A McLean, 'After the belt: school processes in low-exclusion schools', *School Organisation*, 7(3), 1987, pp303-10.
47. Communication from LEAs.

6 Access and choice: pre-school

Quite frankly, I don't think mothers have the same right to work as fathers. If the good Lord had intended us to have equal rights to go out to work, he wouldn't have created man and woman. These are biological facts; young children do depend upon their mothers.'

Patrick Jenkin, *Guardian*, 6 November 1979

Daycare will continue to be primarily a matter of private arrangement between parents and private and voluntary resources except when there are special needs.

John Patten, *Hansard*, 18 March 1985

We have always made it clear that it is not for the government to encourage or discourage women with children to go out to work.

John Major, *Independent*, 21 March 1990

If you have to work you do and if you have to find childcare you find it. When I say 'have' I mean you really want to.

Angela Rumbold, *Family Policy Bulletin*, March 1991

We now turn to a different example of choice and access to education provision. For some, pre-school is largely a private matter for families to decide rather than a sphere for state intervention. Yet many local authorities continue to regard pre-school provision as an important 'compensatory' mechanism for tackling educational disadvantage. Should pre-school be seen as a 'head start' for children, 'early entry' into school, or daycare for working parents?

All-party support for pre-school provision is growing in the 1990s, although there is disagreement as to the merits of different types, and services and funding are fragmented between 'education' and 'care'. The Government seems likely to support expansion, although in what form is not entirely clear. Just before Christmas 1993, John Major promised nursery places for all three and four year olds whose parents wanted it; after nearly a year of agonising over various options, and hints at the party conference, he announced the provision of nursery places 'for all four year olds whose parents wish it'.[1] Other options under discussion include support for playgroups and the voluntary sector (seen as less expensive and supporting parental involvement), helping the private sector and pre-school vouchers (popular with the Tory right wing).[2] But there is strong support for nursery education, as educational arguments for three and four year olds are now generally accepted.[3] (Curiously perhaps, recent official support for pre-school provision came not from the educationalists but from the 'law and order' camp, with the Home Office drawing on evidence of the reduction in juvenile delinquency from the long-term results from the High/Scope pre-school programme in the US, to launch experimental projects in this country.[4])

Although there is likely to be expansion of nursery *education*, there is little government support for publicly funded *daycare* provision for children of working parents. Yet the Government's own figures demonstrate that it is families – particularly lone parents – with young children who are likely to be bringing up their children in poverty, and thus most in need of childcare support. To what extent do education and care services for pre-school children meet the needs of disadvantaged parents and their children?

PRE-SCHOOL – A 'HEAD START' FOR CHILDREN, 'EARLY ENTRY' INTO SCHOOL, OR DAYCARE FOR WORKING PARENTS?

The case for or against pre-school provision depends on arguments over the role women play in the labour force, the role of the state in provision for under-fives, and the effects on young children of care away from their parents (primarily mothers).

Both world wars provided the impetus for childcare to release women into the workforce. As the Minister for Labour, Ernest Bevin, explained in 1941, 'Married women not previously employed [must] supply most of the necessary additional power for industry. From that point of view the provision for the care of children is a matter of first importance to the war effort'.[5] But by 1945, the Ministry of Health was asserting that 'the right policy to pursue would be positively to discourage mothers of children under two from going out to work' and 'to make provision for children between two and five by way of nursery schools and nursery classes'.[6] It is thus not surprising to find a policy of nursery closures following the end of the war as men returned to the workforce. Within a year, the number of day nurseries had dropped to 914; within 20 years only one-third remained open.

In education, priority lay with the statutory school age group during the 1950s and 1960s. Expansion occurred elsewhere – in the self-help playgroup movement, strongly characterised by adult learning and parental involvement, but with its greatest strength in middle class rather than working class areas.[7]

Research in the 1960s on young children's learning opened up the possibility of reducing disadvantage by intervention in the early years – part of the 'War on Poverty' in the US and the compensatory education movement in Britain.[8] This was picked up by the Plowden Report published in 1967, *Children and Their Primary Schools*: 'The value of nursery education in promoting the social development of young children has long been acknowledged. In addition we now know that ... children may also make great educational progress before the age of five.' Mrs Thatcher's 1972 White Paper argued for a programme of nursery expansion, for the first time in the 30 years following the end of the war. Priority was to be given 'in the early stages of the programme to areas of disadvantage'.[9]

Although the White Paper was rapidly dubbed 'the framework for contraction' as government expenditure was squeezed throughout the 1970s and 1980s, there was still some expansion of nursery provision. Expenditure on under-fives by local authorities increased from under 10 per cent of the total spent on primary education in 1979/80 to nearly 20 per cent in 1992/93. But by 1993, only 26 per cent of the under-fives had places in nursery schools or classes (compared with 22 per cent in 1984).[10]

Assumptions about the damage to young children of separation from their mothers have continued to undermine pressure for expansion of daycare. In 1968, a Ministry of Health circular spelling out the criteria for local authority day nurseries restricted places to children 'at risk' and with 'special needs', with the exception of single parents who had 'no option but to go out to work'.[11] Notions of 'good/bad parenting' are still powerful in the family centres which have largely replaced publicly funded day nurseries, catering for families 'at risk' and children 'in need' following the Children Act 1989.[12] This is despite research which shows that all children over the age of one year can benefit from well-run daycare.[13] It remains to be seen whether the Children Act 1989, with its emphasis on a joint approach to 'educational' and 'care' services for children under eight, and its emphasis on a 'pro-active' rather than 'crisis' approach to provision for children and families under stress, will result in any expansion of provision, particularly for disadvantaged children and their families.

CURRENT PROVISION

Britain is still near the bottom of the publicly funded childcare[14] 'league table' compared with its European partners, with 41 per cent of three year olds and 58 per cent of four year olds provided for, compared with almost 100 per cent in Belgium and France at the top of the league.[15] Both public and private childcare services have expanded over the last 30 years. Over the last 30 years, three and four year olds in school (that is, places in nursery classes and places in reception classes in primary schools) rose from 15 per cent to 53 per cent of the age group.[16] Most of the expansion, however, has been in primary schools, as four year olds or 'rising fives' in reception classes;[17] full-time places in nursery schools have actually declined. Day nursery places have also increased (mostly in the private and voluntary sectors[18]) as well as childminders. This shows the rapidly rising demand for full daycare places for children of working parents, a demand which is not met by the statutory sector.

Services are piecemeal and fragmented between the statutory and voluntary or not-for-profit and private sectors, and vary according to region, local authority and neighbourhood, function, age of the child, and socio-economic status of the parents.[19] There is no universal 'blueprint'. Broadly speaking, services cover educational provision for children, daycare for children of parents in employment or education or training, play and care for children and families with 'welfare' needs, and self-help or community-run groups which provide play, education and care for children for short periods of time, as well as support services for parents. It is not always possible to draw clear distinctions between the functions or uses of different types of provision. (Working parents, for example, may use different services, or a combination, to provide care for their children.) But is there equal access to these services?

PROVISION IN SCHOOL

Let us first consider provision in school for the under-fives.[20] Access depends largely on where you live. Provision varies sharply between regions, local authorities, and by type of neighbourhood, ethnic group and social class.[21] Table 6.1 shows the differences between regions in the provision of education for children under five in nursery or primary schools. The north, north west and Yorkshire and Humberside regions remain 'top of the league' for both nursery provision and under-fives in school generally in both 1985 and 1993; while East Anglia, the south east generally and the south west regions remain 'bottom of the league', with the exception of London which has higher proportions of under-fives in both nursery provision and reception classes.

TABLE 6.1: **Education of under-fives in maintained nursery and primary schools – by England regions – 1985 and 1993**

England regions	Nursery schools and classes %		All pupils under five in school* %	
	1985	1993	1985	1993
North	36	44	67	77
Yorks & Humberside	33	40	56	64
North West	27	32	54	64
East Midlands	24	30	42	51
West Midlands	25	29	50	58
East Anglia	9	11	33	37
Greater London	31	34	49	55
Other South East	12	13	23	31
South West	7	9	31	37

Source: DES/DFE, *Statistical Bulletins* 10/86 and 6/94

*includes children in local authority nursery schools and nursery classes in primary schools, and four year olds and 'rising fives' in primary school reception classes

These inequalities are even more pronounced if we look at local authorities rather than regions. The map of pre-school provision suggests that local authorities serving more disadvantaged regions have made determined efforts to develop 'compensatory provision' through nursery schools and classes.

Nursery inequalities

In January 1993, 'under-fives' in Gloucestershire had no opportunity to attend nursery schools or classes, although 32 per cent of the age group got into school before the statutory age. But in Cleveland, 57 per cent of the age group was in nursery schools or classes in primary schools, with an additional 35 per cent already in school – the highest proportion in the shire counties. In metropolitan districts, 60 per cent of under-fives in Walsall were in nursery schools or classes, and a further 34 per cent in school; while in Bromley only 2 per cent had the chance of a nursery school or class and only 18 per cent got into school early.

Department for Education, *Statistical Bulletin 6/94*

DAYCARE

The development of daycare provision has had lower priority than educational provision and is even more patchy. For parents with young children who are working or trying to get a job, childcare is essential – and especially for lone parents (who are predominantly women). Workplace nurseries are used by only 1 per cent of families for their under-fives.[22] These are most likely to be found in high-status firms rather than in the low-paid, part-time work for women that has mushroomed over the past decade. Two hours twice a week at a playgroup is not much help for parents in this position.

In a recent survey of unemployment in Oxfordshire, just under half the parents interviewed needed some kind of support with their children to enable them to return to work; three quarters preferred care located near their home; 12 per cent wanted workplace nurseries. Seventeen per cent of those interviewed had wanted to take a course but had not done so because there was no childcare provision.[23] The 1980 *Women and Employment Survey* showed that women lose 25-50 per cent of potential lifetime earnings through bringing up a family. Much of this is related to lack of childcare. Men's employment experience and earnings are largely unaffected by fatherhood.[24]

Again, Britain lags behind much of Europe in its daycare

arrangements. Comparative figures published in 1990 show that 2 per cent of children under three in the UK used publicly funded childcare services compared with 20 per cent in Belgium and France and 48 per cent in Denmark.[25]

WHAT WORKING WOMEN WANT

Childcare of all kinds is in heavy demand. But the striking fact is that most children with working mothers are looked after by family or friends. The picture in 1990 is still more or less the same as it was in 1980:[26] relatives are by far the most important providers of childcare for working women. In the British Social Attitudes Survey,[27] 64 per cent of the working women interviewed had their under-fives looked after by relatives, whatever their preferences. When they used out-of-home services, childminders and day nurseries filled the gap.

What working women want

- One in five working women prefer to send their under-fives to a workplace nursery if they can – perhaps to have them near at work.
- 11 per cent choose a 'mother's help' or a nanny to look after them at home.
- 8 per cent choose a childminder.
- 14 per cent vote equally for local authority or private day nurseries.
- Yet childcare for children of working women is still largely a private matter, relying mainly on family.

British Social Attitudes: the 8th report, 1991

The lack of childcare provision is likely to hit poor families particularly hard – partly because of the costs of private provision and partly because of the absence of publicly funded services. This is especially the case for lone parents, who are likely to be found in the poorest groups.[28] Many would be in employment but for lack of childcare or, if they are employed, would have to give up work if their childcare arrangements stopped.[29] Yet lone mothers with pre-school children are even less likely than married mothers to be earning: the percentage in either full-time or part-time work dropped during the 1980s and early 1990s, while the percentage of both full-time and part-time married mothers in work has increased, as we can see from Table 6.2.

TABLE 6.2: **Need for childcare: mothers with children under five by part-time and full-time employment (England only)**

Women with 0-4 year olds	1981	1991
Lone mothers		
numbers	104,375	323,485
economically active	29.3%	25.7%
working	21.4%	19.3%
full-time	10%	8.2%
part-time	11.4%	10%
self-employed	n/a	1.1%
'Couple' mothers		
numbers	1,857,657	1,786,586
economically active	25%	45%
working	22.5%	41.3%
full-time	5.9%	11.4%
part-time	16.6%	26%
self-employed	n/a	3.9%

Source: *Census* 1981 and 1991

Working-class families are less likely than professional families to use pre-school services anyway, especially non-statutory provision such as playgroups or childminders[30] – probably on grounds of cost. Again, women with higher levels of education are more likely to be using childcare[31] – not surprising, as better qualified women are more likely to be working, and in higher paid jobs.

Government response to pressure for expansion has largely been in the form of encouragement for employer-led initiatives, for example, with the removal in the 1991 Budget of the tax liability on employees using workplace nurseries (previously regarded as a 'taxable perk'). This, however, tends to benefit highly paid women in top companies, where employers have realised that losing experienced and trained workers when they start a family may be more expensive in the long run than the costs of setting up daycare; it does little for the low paid or part-timers. Workplace nurseries provide for a fraction of the work force. There was an unsuccessful attempt to persuade the Government to extend this tax concession to all forms of pre-school provision in the 1992 Budget.

Childcare in poor areas may be more difficult to find, not least because of the cost of private daycare. The 1993 Budget was hailed as a breakthrough, with its £40 allowance for childcare for poor working parents. However, the small print revealed this to be no 'pre-school voucher' – rather, a limited 'disregard' from October 1994 for *some* parents on *some* welfare benefits with a child under 11 who has a nursery or childminder place. DSS estimates claim that up to 150,000 families will benefit, with some 50,000 claimants taking up work as a result of the measure and some 100,000 existing claimants receiving more benefit. However, in the context of the complex family credit calculation, the maximum £40 'allowance' actually translates to a maximum of £28 a week, considerably less than the average childminder costs of £1.41 per hour in 1991.[32] It remains to be seen whether these limited measures will either encourage more employers to set up provision or enable unemployed claimants to return to work.

The conclusion must be that, although publicly funded educational provision is expanding slowly, childcare in general in Britain, both 'education' and 'care', continues to be patchy and uneven, and largely a matter of privately funded services and 'informal' care. Many parents put together 'packages' of care for their pre-school children, using both statutory and voluntary sources, and family and friends. For lone parents, this seems to be considerably more difficult. Yet we know that these are precisely the people who are likely to be bringing up their children in poverty.

NOTES

1. Quoted in *New Statesman and Society*, 4 November 1994.
2. *Times Educational Supplement*, 7 and 14 October 1994, 4 November 1994.
3. K Sylva, 'The impact of early learning on children's later development', in C Ball, *Start Right: the importance of early learning*, Royal Society for the Encouragement of Arts, Manufacture and Commerce, 1994; National Commission on Education, *Learning to Succeed: a radical look at education today and a strategy for the future*, Heinemann, 1993, Chapter 6.
4. L J Schweinhart, H V Barnes and D P Weikart, *Significant Benefits: the High/Scope Perry Pre-school Study through age 27*, High/Scope Press, 1993; D Utting, J Bright and C Henricson, *Crime and the Family: improving child-rearing and preventing delinquency*, Family Policy Studies Centre/ NACRO/Crime Concern, 1993.
5. Quoted in H Penn and K A Riley, *Managing Services for the Under-Fives*, Longman, 1992, p4.

6. Quoted in *ibid*, p5.
7. C Owen and P Moss: 'Patterns of pre-school provision in English local authorities', *Journal of Educational Policy*, 4(4), 1989, pp309-28.
8. G Smith (ed), *Educational Priority: Vol 4: The West Riding Project*, HMSO, 1975.
9. Department of Education and Science, *Education: a framework for expansion*, HMSO, 1972, para 28.
10. Department for Education, *Statistical Bulletin 6/94*, DFE, June 1994.
11. Ministry of Health, *Daycare Facilities for Children Under Five*, Circular 37/68, 1968.
12. T Smith, 'Family centres, children in need and the Children Act 1989', in J Gibbons (ed), *The Children Act 1989 and Family Support: principles into practice*, HMSO, 1992; W van der Eyken, *Day Nurseries in Action: a national study of local authority day nurseries in England 1975-1983*, Department of Child Health, University of Bristol, Mimeo, 1984.
13. K Sylva, *op cit*; E Melhuish and P Moss, *Daycare for Young Children: international perspectives*, Routledge, 1991; C Howes, 'Can the age of entry into childcare and the quality of childcare predict adjustment in the kindergarten?', *Developmental Psychology*, 26(2), 1990, pp292-303.
14. The terms 'childcare' and 'pre-school' are used in this chapter to refer to all out-of-home provision for pre-school aged children, whether 'educational' or 'care' in type and provided by statutory, voluntary or private sectors.
15. P Moss, 'Statistics on early childhood services: placing Britain in an international context', in Ball, *op cit*. These percentages would be higher if privately funded services (playgroups, childminders and day nurseries in the voluntary and private sectors) were included, as they are in some government statistics.
16. *Social Trends* 24, 1994; Table 3.2. This is in both the state and the private sectors in the UK; the proportion in state schools only would be slightly lower.
17. Department for Education, *Statistical Bulletin*, issue No. 6/94, DFE, June 1994.
18. Between 1980/81 and 1991/92, the number of day nurseries provided by local authorities actually fell from 32,000 to 30,000, while in the voluntary and private sectors the number of nurseries is estimated to have more than quadrupled from 23,000 to 105,000. Playgroups also increased over the decade, but less significantly (433,000 to 496,000), although they still serve the largest number of children aged 0 to 4. The increase in registered childminders (from 110,000 to 297,000) again reflects the demand for full-time daycare by working parents (*Social Trends 24*, 1994, Table 3.2).
19. H Meltzer, *Daycare Services for Children: a survey carried out on behalf of the Department of Health in 1990*, OPCS, HMSO, 1994; Moss, *op cit*; Owen

and Moss, *op cit*; Penn and Riley, *op cit.*

20. That is, nursery schools, nursery classes in primary school, and four year olds and 'rising fives' in primary school reception classes.
21. M Bone, *Pre-school Children and the Need for Daycare*, OPCS, HMSO, 1977; B Cohen, *Caring for Children: services and policies for childcare and equal opportunities in the United Kingdom*, Report for the European Commission's Childcare Network, Commission of the European Communities, 1988; B Cohen and F Fraser, *Childcare in a Modern Welfare System: towards a new national policy*, Institute for Public Policy Research, 1991; Department for Education, *Statistical Bulletin*, issue No. 6/94, DFE, June 1994; A F Osborn, N R Butler and A C Morris, *The Social Life of Britain's Five Year Olds. A report of the Child Health and Education Study*, Routledge and Kegan Paul, 1984.
22. A Bridgewood and D Savage, *General Household Survey 1991*, OPCS, HMSO, 1993.
23. M Emmerich and J Lewis, *Unemployment in Oxfordshire*, CLES European Research Network Ltd, 1991, pp56, 80, 96ff.
24. H Joshi, 'The cost of caring', in C Glendinning and J Millar (eds), *Women and Poverty in Britain in the 1990s*, Harvester Wheatsheaf, 1992; H Joshi, 'Sex and motherhood as handicaps in the labour market', in M Maclean and D Groves (eds), *Women's Issues in Social Policy*, Routledge, 1991.
25. Commission of the European Communities, *Childcare in Europe 1985-1990*, CEC, 1990. These figures exclude playgroups, on the grounds that average attendance is only five hours a week and that playgroups receive minimal public funds. Quoted in Cohen and Fraser, *op cit*, p44.
26. J Martin and C Roberts, *Women and Employment: a lifetime perspective. The report of the 1980 DE/OPCS Women and Employment Survey*, HMSO, 1984.
27. S Witherspoon and G Prior, 'Working mothers: free to choose?', in R Jowell, L Brook and S Taylor (eds), *British Social Attitudes: the 8th report*, Dartmouth/ SCPR, 1991.
28. Department of Social Security, *Households Below Average Income. a statistical analysis 1979-1990/91*, HMSO, 1993.
29. J Bradshaw and J Millar, *Lone Parent Families in the UK*, DSS Research Report 6, HMSO, 1991.
30. *General Household Survey 1986*, OPCS, HMSO.
31. A Bridgewood and D Savage, *op cit.*
32. DSS Press Release 93/214, 1 December 1993: 'Peter Lilley announces boost for working families'; Child Poverty Action Group, *Welfare Rights Bulletin 121*, August 1994, p6; Unemployment Unit and Youthaid, *Working Brief 50*, January 1994, p11.

III
The real costs of education

Education has never been completely free at the point of delivery. Despite a number of legislative safeguards, there are growing costs which parents have to bear on a weekly basis. As with indirect taxation, these constitute a disproportionate burden on the poorest familes. Our central argument is that such costs constitute a major barrier to learning.

In the next two chapters we draw on two postal surveys carried out in early summer 1993 in LEAs and a sample of primary and secondary schools. We illustrate our arguments about the 'real' costs of education with material from a number of in-depth interviews with parents.

7 The costs of 'free education'

Education 'free to all' remains a basic principle.[1] Both the 1944 Education Act and the legislation of the 1980s explicitly prohibit education authorities or schools from charging for educational activities, but there remains scope for 'voluntary contributions' as well as a good deal of ambiguity over the definition of 'curricular activities'. In this chapter, we draw extensively on our surveys to explore the current reality of some of these costs in practice for children in low income families. In particular, we look at the cost of school clothing, transport to school, school trips and of staying on at school.

SCHOOL CLOTHING

Whether or not schools require a uniform, the provision of appropriate school clothing is a major cost to parents. One way in which poorer parents have been helped in this area is in the provision of school clothing grants.

Although there is a continuing legal obligation for schools or LEAs to provide meals at least for those children entitled to free meals, no such obligation exists or has ever existed for school clothing grants.[2] School Clothing Grants or School Uniform Grants are discretionary.[3] Having decided on provision, it is then up to LEAs (or schools, if this function has been delegated to them) to determine eligibility. If grants are provided, there may be rules governing entitlement, or the allocation of a grant may be entirely discretionary and based on the judgement of the teacher or educational welfare officer.

Given the entirely discretionary nature of the payments, one might expect many authorities to have abandoned such schemes. However, 85 per cent of the authorities in our survey reported that they still gave clothing grants. In the main, these grants continued to be made at LEA level. Out of our respondent LEAs, only one devolved this function to schools.

There was, however, wide variation in the generosity of such schemes as to both criteria for eligibility, frequency, and amount of payment.

TABLE 7.1: **Numbers of clothing grants given by respondent LEAs in the three years ending July 1993**

	Minimum	Maximum	Median
1990/91	158	29,357	6,876
1991/92	2	34,294	7,172
1992/93	2	69,971	10,161

Although the number of grants awarded has increased in the past three years, the amount of the awards has, despite inflation, remained more or less at the same level.

TABLE 7.2: **Size of clothing grants given by respondent LEAs in the three years ending July 1993**

	Minimum £	Maximum £	Mean £
1990/91	15	64	33
1991/92	12	79	34
1992/93	12	71	34

Some authorities reported a recent cutback in grants or their availability:

> Prior to April '93 all pupils whose parents were in receipt of income support or family credit were eligible for a bi-annual grant of £30 for the secondary phase. Post April 1993, grant is made available to pupils in dire need to enable them to attend school.

Where they exist, school clothing grants may be given in cash, vouchers or (rarely) in kind. Many authorities in the Yorkshire/ Lancashire/Greater Manchester area operate issues of clothing from a central store set up specifically for the purpose:

> A means-tested system. Primary-aged children receive two items, secondary-age, three items on admission to secondary school. All items are provided through a central store operated by the Yorkshire Purchasing Organisation. Parents and children attend on an appointment basis.

Others issue vouchers:

> Grants are provided in the form of a book of vouchers. These are posted to the applicant together with a list of shops in this Borough that accept them.
>
> Vouchers provided to family on DSS benefits every three years. £35, £35, £90 (11+), £35 emergency schemes and special needs boarding scheme provide additional assistance in case by case basis.
>
> A means-tested benefit up to a set figure above basic living needs ranging from £20 to £30 depending on the age of the child. Payments are by voucher, one voucher per child. Redeemable at certain stores, eg, C&A, BHS, etc.

One authority had different arrangements for primary and secondary schools:

> Primary pupils do not receive grants. They select items from LEA clothing store, ie, coat/blazer/skirt/trousers shoes.

We asked local authorities which did not currently make grants whether they had made such grants in the past and when grants ceased to be available. Of the seven LEAs who reported that they had stopped giving clothing grants, most ceased to do so in the late 1970s or early 1980s – victims of earlier rounds of expenditure cuts.

We also asked if there were any other schemes to provide clothing operating in conjunction with the local authority. Some reported links with charities, eg,

> Payments for clothing and student grants to widows/widowers whose children are in full-time education.

Schools were also asked about arrangements to meet financial difficulties in providing for school clothing. Almost *all* schools responding operated some form of second-hand shop for school clothing, irrespective of whether there was any system of clothing grants in operation:

> PTA Nearly New Shop; items are provided by the school at a reduced rate or free in cases of perceived need.
>
> We sell school uniform at cost (ie, sweatshirt £7) and there are PTA sales, etc. (Second-hand clothing does not go well in this school.)
>
> School stock of clothing – grants for school fund in exceptional cases.
>
> Matron sells second-hand clothing and items occasionally given free in hardship cases.
>
> School runs a second-hand shop and it also uses money to support real need from a Benevolent Fund. We want all in uniform so we put up the money where necessary.
>
> School has a stock of clothing, but most pupils refuse to wear it and actually have the correct clothes at home.
>
> Second-hand uniforms sold, payment in instalments, payment from School Fund.

A charity created 100 years ago to buy boots and clothing for poor children in Coventry is providing growing numbers of pupils in the city with new shoes. The Coventry Children's Boot Fund, thought to be the only one of its kind in the country, bought 400 pairs of new shoes for schoolchildren during the past year, compared with about 300 pairs in the late 1980s. It expects demand to increase further during 1993 – its centenary year.

Times Educational Supplement, 8 January 1993

GETTING TO SCHOOL

The Education Act of 1944 laid the foundation of principles, which remain intact today, regarding the provision of free school transport. These hold that 'distance' rather than 'financial' criteria determine who gets free transport and who does not. Children living beyond what is defined as 'walking distance' from school (two miles for under eight year olds and three miles for older pupils) are entitled to free transport, lest travelling expenses should preclude them from regular attendance. Local authorities are duty bound to make such provision. However, initiatives subsequent to the Act to introduce a financial qualifier for free transport, whereby there would be a national flat-rate fare for those living nearer to school, have not so far succeeded.

Beyond this, however, LEAs may use their own discretion in helping children who live nearer to school. Since school transport costs may constitute a regular expense for many families, and a particular burden on poor families, our survey of LEAs asked whether they operated any discretionary schemes to help with the travel costs of pupils living within the statutory distance from school. Thirty-one of the 45 authorities responding said they did offer such schemes. These varied from subsidised fares for all children, to free travel or concessionary rates for some, but the targeting criterion was not often financial need as such. Priority for help with travel costs was more commonly given on grounds of special health or educational needs, or on the basis of risk attached to the route to school. Though some authorities did earmark travel funds for children from families on income support or low income, it appeared that the cost of getting children to and from school, within the statutory distance, is most often met by parents, regardless of their means.

VOLUNTARY CONTRIBUTIONS AND CHARGING POLICIES

So far, our discussion of the costs to parents of sending their children to school has centred around the most visible expenses – clothing children at school and transporting them to and fro. We argue in this and the next chapter that the extent and sensitivity with which the burden of these costs have been addressed or mitigated is far from satisfactory. Nonetheless, these expenses have at least been recognised formally and met with a response in policy and law. To focus on them exclusively, however, is to obscure a range of other costs routinely incurred by parents supporting children at school with which they may receive only ad hoc or sporadic help, if any at all. In the present climate of both recession and locally managed schools (LMS), it is likely that these costs are becoming more burdensome and stigmatising for families with limited means.

Charging for Education

Section 61 of the 1944 Act expressly prohibited 'any school maintained by a local education authority' from charging fees either for admission or 'in respect of the education provided'. In practice this left LEAs and schools with a wide discretion to provide free 'curricular' trips – even if these were residential in nature. A system of significant cross subsidisation of 'extra curricular' activities also developed.

From 1 April 1989 charging policies were tightened up. LEAs were required to produce policy statements on charging for school activities and the legislation itself was much more prescriptive on just what could or could not be charged for. The legislation continued to prohibit charging for the supply of books and materials and for 'non residential' school trips. However, it now became possible to charge for individual music lessons, the board and lodging element of 'residential trips' and 'optional extras' and activities taking place outside school hours. Any charges so levied must be remitted for children whose parents are on family credit or income support.

The legislation[4] provoked LEAs into considering all aspects of their charging policy. In particular, the practice of asking for 'voluntary contributions' for items which could not be charged for was considered by many LEAs. One LEA, in a letter sent to schools in February 1989, stated that 'the School Policy Statement should make clear to parents that it is quite within the law for schools to request voluntary contributions for the benefit of the school or in support of any school activity, whether *during or outside* school hours, residential or non-residential. The size of the voluntary contribution does not have to be linked to the actual cost of the activity...' Although the letter went on to stress that pupils whose parents did not contribute should be treated no differently, this is an area which causes great problems to children of poor parents. The following comments from parents in respect of 'curricular' school trips illustrate the point:

> *...but you've still got to give 'em pocket money. My daughter had a trip not long ago. And er ... it said voluntary. But I did write back saying yes she can go on it but how much pocket money does she need? A fiver! I haven't got a fiver spare to give 'er. So she couldn't go on it. My kids don't go on school trips.*

*Yet if it's a small trip where they all go, all the class is expected to go, then they will say well if you can't afford it then ... just pay a little something towards it or something.[*Have you ever done that?*] No I just say I can't afford it and then in the end they take 'em anyway.*

However, the following quote shows that there is confusion as to how 'voluntary' these contributions are:

Well yeah ... they're sometimes really nice ... (the school secretary) she's really nice and if I ... if I really can't afford say ... then she'll just leave it and say oh pay later ... but if she wasn't there then...

Even where school trips are not and never have been free (for example, trips abroad), parents described these increasingly as a part of the agenda of school activities, and one in which their children hoped and expected to participate. Ranging from local day outings to trips abroad, these were often prohibitively expensive even when subsidised. This was especially the case when there was more than one child to take into consideration:

My boy's fourteen and I've had a lot of pressure on his ... trips going away for a week ... and they're costing over £100 ... Yeah ... for him to go ... £80 or £90. And I mean that's a lot money when ... I mean I've only got two children at school now as opposed to three ... but you feel obliged then to let your other one go because he's gone ... so you're talking ... you know he possibly will be going somewhere with his school in the last year...

Parents felt pressured to enable their children to go, and were often as disappointed as the child that they could not afford to send them:

That's another thing that I ... I couldn't afford to send my son to what he wanted to do ... this time. And I just had to say no. Cos I couldn't afford it. He wanted to go to Boulogne and ... for the day ... that was about 30 odd pound for the day. And I just couldn't do it. So it disappointed him but ... he just had to realise that we couldn't afford it.

We like them to go ... but we still find it quite difficult to send them ... you know sort of £80 is quite a bit of money for about four days. I know it's good for them ... it does 'em good and its brilliant but it still ... seems to me to be a lot of money ... you know so I mean that's another thing that ... you get a lot of pressure on cos they seem to be having more and more of these trips each year.

When schools could legitimately charge under the 1988 Act then financial help was sometimes available to parents on income support or family credit, but not to others whose budget was nonetheless tight:

> *They do ... they do offer. But I mean I've never got it because my husband's working. Well you know it's ... if you're on social, family credit and that sort thing that's the way you get it ... It is embarrassing having to ask for something isn't it?*

Where schools might offer support, this was generally done on an informal, somewhat unpredictable basis. This often meant that parents had to take the initiative in asking for assistance, which fed into their sense of embarrassment and reluctance to ask:

> *Oh yeah I hate not paying ... not being able to pay ... I hate having to ask ... I always try and pay ... I wouldn't want 'em to say oh you didn't ... your mum and dad didn't pay nothing...*

Not infrequently, it appears that faced with inadequate, unpredictable and stigmatising support, parents who could, turned to their own informal networks for help:

> *I'd be very embarrassed. I would ... because I'd hate to think that one of 'em had to miss out because I didn't have the money ... But then I'm lucky because I've got family and I could ... borrow ... you know if ... well then some people haven't got any family and I ... should imagine that a lot of children do ... on that borderline a lot of children do miss out ... because their parents quite ... can't quite afford it ... whereas I'm lucky because I can borrow it off you know people anyway.*

A second routine and significant expenditure mentioned to us by parents was the cost of providing their children with materials and equipment necessary for the curriculum. It appears that parents are increasingly being required to furnish their children with everything from specialist art materials or fancy cooking ingredients down to the basics of pens, pencils and exercise books. Under the 1988 Act[5] (as under s61 of the 1944 Act) this is clearly illegal. It may well be that schools framed their requests as voluntary contributions, as the following example illustrates:

> The college enters some 400 students for the English Literature GCSE exam each year. The cost of providing set books is in the region of £10 per student and, of course, because they may be annotated, they can only be used once. We will therefore have to find an extra £4,000 per year. We are writing to ask for your help in providing these books. We

are asking for a donation of £5 per student ... If there is any difficulty in paying, please ask your son or daughter to see ... to come to an alternative arrangement. This will, of course, be kept confidential.

A community college in the Midlands

However, this was not the perception of parents. According to the parents we spoke to, these requests constituted a major drain on resources on top of all the other expenses of maintaining their children at school. Worse, it was never ending, since supplies were forever running out, getting spoiled or lost:

Yes ... (it is getting) more expensive ... cos if her book's finished I have to buy them a new book ... I mean the last one she had I think that was a ... you know the A4 paper, about £1.10 for that ... that's both of them I have to buy it for. You have to buy ... they have to have fountain pens now! So that's three I have to buy fountain pens for ... And she's terrible cos she really presses down and she ... all the bit [ie, nib] goes on it and everything. We're forever buying her a new one.

I just spent 25 (pounds) last week that was on their pens, their pencils, the pencil sharpeners, the rubbers ... and they gotta have it ... and we've had to go out and ... spend all that ... I couldn't believe it. When I got to the till ... and it didn't look a lot there ... and she said 'twenty-four eighty-five', [whispers] 'Has she got that wrong? she must have got it wrong.' They've gotta 'em all have glue as well. Yeah the 15 and the 12 year old I have to buy glue for 'em. And I got out ... I couldn't believe it. I was going in the car and I'm saying was it ... are you sure it cost that? Sure it was that? And he said I don't know. And we got home and I calculated it all up and it was right. I couldn't believe it.

Again, rather than let their children go without, some parents fell back on their own families for support:

The amount she has to pay for art stuff is ... tremendous ... They've (school) got it but ... like ... if you want to get on then you've got to take your own stuff ... She has to have special oiled paper or whatever they call it ... and that was 10 (pounds) something for about four sheets ... And then they've got paint brushes which she has to have different sizes so she's got to have a pack with about 10 ... Then she has to have the charcoal of different sizes, then the pencils of different sizes, then the oil paints and the water paints. I said she needs some paints and then my mum come up and says oh I've got these water colours from somewhere ... um ... I don't particularly need them ... but you know she's gone out and bought them special.

Parents' reports also suggest that schools were not always as sensitive as they might be to the financial strain imposed by these demands. Some simply issued lists of things children were required to have, without suggested alternatives or economies; some were positively wasteful of parents' limited resources:

> *My oldest son ... he was doing pizza. She wrote down all these different herbs he had to have ... things we never ... we could have quite happily enjoyed that pizza without those herbs. But he had to have 'em. So I had to go out and spend a fortune on all these different herbs ... and ... they're in the cupboard now ... They never really got ... cos my kids are a basic ... they're not fancy eaters they like ... like basic meat and two veg kids. So all this garlic and herbs and that was um ... a waste. Whereas if they had one pot at school, and give it all (a measure of mixed herbs) for 10 pence or something, that would have been great.*

Beyond their acute awareness of how much all this cost and how little they could afford it, several parents were struck by a sense of the injustice of having to pay at all. They recognised, rightly, that these had been provisions to which they, as children, had been entitled for free:

> *It's worse than it used to be. We never ... when I was at school we never paid for anything, whereas now you have to pay for everything ... if they lose a book you have to pay 25 pence to get another one.*

Likewise, the demands upon parents were not just to pay for the materials of their own child's education, but to contribute to equipping and sustaining the school itself:

> *They're always after money for their own school. They're never got enough money ... you know ... books ... Fund-raising for the school ... I don't remember that years ago. No but then ... I don't blame the school. I blame the government for not giving them the money. I mean when we was at school, you never heard ... you never used to have sales and fetes and things did you? Cakes and things ... to raise money for the school?*

Our findings echo the national picture. A survey conducted by the National Confederation of Parent Teacher Associations (NCPTA) in 1990 showed parents contributing £55 million to schools – about 27 per cent of the normal capitation allowance in primary schools and 7 per cent in secondary schools. This represented a more than threefold increase for primary schools when compared to a similar survey in 1985. With less money coming to schools from LEAs, the situation will have worsened. As the NCPTA report concludes:

> A state education system should be equally accessible to all children and success or otherwise should not depend on the ability of parents to pay.[6]

STAYING ON AT SCHOOL

DISCRETIONARY AWARDS AND GRANTS

Increasing numbers of young people of school-leaving age are facing poor employment prospects and are opting to stay on at school or college between the ages of 16 and 18. There are two sources of financial provision potentially available to support those from low-income families in doing so. The first, Educational Maintenance Allowances (EMAs), are provided by LEAs on a discretionary means-tested basis, for students staying on at school; the second, further education (FE) awards, are made on a similar basis, for those continuing their education at sixth form college.

A report by CPAG in 1983[7] drew attention to the fact that while most LEAs ran EMA and/or FE award schemes, their discretionary nature meant that there was wide variation in the percentages of young people receiving them. Recent national figures for 1991/92[8] reiterate this message. Of the 116 education authorities in England and Wales, 99 ran EMA schemes and 90 issued FE awards. Our own postal survey of 47 education authorities in 1993 presents a similar picture. However, according to the Department for Education figures, the rates of provision varied widely across authorities and regional averages. Regionally, EMA rates (per 1000 of the 16 and 17 year old population) ranged from averages of 74 in Wales and 60 in Inner and Greater London, to just 11 in the rest of the south east. Rates of FE awards were equally varied; the north west and Yorkshire with Humberside provided 127 and 126 per 1,000 respectively, while East Anglia was lowest with 33. More recent data collected by the National Foundation for Educational Research (NFER)[9] suggest that the numbers of both EMA and FE awards increased in 1992/93. Projections for 1993/94 suggest a further increase in numbers of FE awards but a slight decrease in EMAs. However, such increases are not 'across the board' – there was a trend for LEAs which gave a high proportion of a discretionary award (EMA or FE) per capita in 1990/91 to give a high proportion in 1992/93, and those giving lower proportions in 1990/91 to give the same in 1992/93.

The NFER study confirms our own findings – that there is wide variation across LEAs in the size of EMA and FE award budgets, and in the amounts paid. The NFER estimates the average EMA award to have been about £440 pa in 1991/92. What is much less clear is how well, or poorly, such provisions meet the need for which they are intended. This applies both to the pattern of their distribution and to the sums of money provided. Certainly, our own survey suggested that both budget allocations and the levels of award have suffered under the recent climate of stringency in public spending. Though some authorities spoke of increasing the rate of minor FE awards over discretionary awards for higher education, many spoke of freezes or cuts in total budget, resulting in reduced awards to cope with increased demand. All this points to major disadvantage for children from low-income families wishing to pursue study beyond the age of 16.

SUMMARY

In this and the next chapter, we use evidence from our own surveys to question whether education can be considered 'free for all' – and particularly for children from low-income families. The answer must surely be 'no', in significant respects. There are clearly costs associated with feeding and clothing children at school, and getting them there. But there are also more 'hidden' costs in the shape of 'voluntary contributions' – on which, as we have seen in Chapter 4, schools increasingly rely for the substance, not merely the 'frills', of education. There are also structural disadvantages built into the system of awards for post-16 education. All of this bears particularly heavily on children from low-income families.

NOTES

1. This chapter and the following one build on previous work published by CPAG and, in particular, David Bull's 1980 pamphlet, *What Price 'Free' Education?*
2. See Bull, *op cit*, p35.
3. Under s81 of the 1944 Act. The distinction between distinctive clothing grants – that is, school uniform grants – and other school clothing grants was important when local education authority expenditure had to be 'approved' by central government. This is no longer the case.

4. 1988 Education Reform Act, ss106-111.
5. Section 106.
6. National Confederation of Parent Teacher Associations, *The State of Schools in England and Wales*, NCPTA, 1991.
7. L Burghes and R Stagles, *No Choice at 16: a study of educational maintenance allowances*, CPAG, 1983.
8. Department for Education, *Statistical Bulletin 22/93, Student Awards in England and Wales*, DFE, 1993.
9. F Fletcher-Campbell, W Keys and L Kendall, *Discretionary award provision in England and Wales*, Calouste Gulbenkian Foundation, 1994.

8 School meals

Since the last century, concern for children's health and nutritional standards has formed part of the education service's wider 'welfare' function, as we saw in Chapter 2. The school meals service had its origins in 1879 when the Manchester School Board provided meals for 'destitute and badly nourished children'.[1] Other school boards followed suit and the Education Act of 1906 confirmed earlier ad hoc arrangements by giving local authorities the power to provide meals at an economic price and to remit charges in the case of needy children.

Under the 1944 Education Act,[2] every local education authority had an obligation to provide 'milk, meals and other refreshments' in schools which they maintained. The meals could be provided at a charge but this was fixed uniformly across the country. With the advent of national assistance in 1948, children whose parents were in receipt of the benefit (later supplementary benefit) were entitled to free meals. When family income supplement (FIS) was introduced in 1970, this, too, 'passported' free school meals. Local authorities had further discretionary power to provide free meals for other low-income groups.

The Education Act 1980 signalled the first major changes in the school meals service for 35 years. Under this Act the obligation to provide school meals contained in the 1944 Act was removed, except in the case of children entitled to free meals (at that time, those whose parents were in receipt of supplementary benefit or FIS). If local authorities chose to continue to provide a universal service, the 1980 Act allowed them to make such charge for it as was thought to be reasonable. This meant that the nationally fixed, subsidised price came to an end. From a fixed price across the country of 25p per meal in 1979, there was a variation by 1981 between a low of 35p and a high of 60p.[3] This legislation therefore marked a watershed. It introduced geographic variation in school meal prices – a trend which has become more marked in recent years following the introduction of local management of schools (LMS). Moreover, the 1980 Act saw the abandonment of the national nutritional standards introduced by regulations under the 1944 Act.

The Social Security Act 1986, coming into force in April 1988, introduced two important changes to the availability of free meals. First, it provided that children whose parents received family credit (the successor to FIS) could not receive free school meals (or free welfare milk). Second, by amending s22 of the Education Act 1980, it abolished the discretionary power of local authorities to provide free meals for children from low-income families. The effect was that only those children whose parents were in receipt of income support (the successor to supplementary benefit) could receive free meals. It was argued in the White Paper that preceded the Act that curtailing availability of free meals to family credit recipients was compensated by an increase in the level of the benefit. However, no precise details were given. As CPAG pointed out in its response to the Green Paper which first introduced the changes, average meal prices varied widely throughout the country. CPAG warned that, 'unless compensation equals the highest school meal price, some poor families on family credit will lose from the switch.'[4] In fact, the level of compensation for both free meals *and* welfare milk was £2.55 a week per child in April 1988.[5] There are around 190 school days a year. If we ignore the fact that the 'compensation' was also intended to cover milk, this works out as compensation for meals at 70p a day. Seventeen shire counties were charging more than this in the autumn of 1988. Poor families in these areas suffered substantial cuts.

The Education Reform Act 1988 added further complexity to the school meals service. The introduction of LMS and of grant maintained schools has meant that, in some LEAs, the school meals service has been devolved to schools.

Following the policy changes during the 1980s, several questions arise concerning low-income families and access for their children to the school meals service.

- To what extent is there a universal service available? If the service is only residuary for children from families on income support, it will not only be stigmatising *per se* for the recipient children, but will also deny other low-income children access to (potentially) subsidised food.

- How much are meals and to what extent are they subsidised? The availability of low-cost meals is very important for low-income families not on income support.
- To what extent do families fail to take up entitlement to free meals and what are the reasons for this?
- Are free meals administered both at the LEA and school level in such a way as to reduce or eliminate stigma?

To answer these questions we carried out surveys in LEAs, in a sample of schools and with parents.

THE IMPORTANCE OF SCHOOL MEALS FOR THOSE LIVING ON A LOW INCOME

In 1980 the Black Report summarised evidence in relation to the importance on health grounds of school meals.[6] The conclusions were unequivocal: children – especially those from low-income households – relied on school meals for nutrients important to growth and 'any reduction in the provision of school meals would mean putting at risk the development of significant numbers of children'.[7] Although the report has never been accepted by Conservative governments, Black was in this respect following one of the findings of the Cockerill Working Party on nutrition in schools set up by the Heath Government. Reporting in 1975, it asserted that it was 'not safe to assume that all children necessarily receive a satisfactory diet at home'.[8]

The importance of the school meal for children from poor families is predicated on the assumption that such meals are of high nutritional standard. While it is outside the scope of this chapter to consider nutritional standards in detail,[9] it is crucial to acknowledge two policy threads which have conspired to reduce standards. First, the development of the cash cafeteria in the late 1970s. Introduced on grounds of 'choice', it allows the selection by children of nutritionally poor meals. Moreover, the cash allocation to those on a low income often allows only a nutritionally poor meal to be purchased:

> *My two oldest ... they have ... they have like, um, a ticket, but the ticket only buys 'em one pound five p [£1.05] ... and out of that all they have is like maybe a roll and p'raps a packet of crisps and that's it. That's the 1.05p gone. You don't get a drink from it.*

Second, following the Education Act 1980, which allowed the abandonment of a universal service and the provision of a residuary service to those entitled to free meals 'as appears to the authority requisite', standards could be implicitly reduced. We shall return to both these points later.

Notwithstanding the regrettable policy changes which have threatened nutritional standards, a recent report from the Social Security Research Unit (SSRU) at the Institute of Education suggests that meals in primary schools are worth defending – 83 per cent of schools surveyed provided meals of average or very good quality.[10]

THE OVERALL PICTURE

During the past four years the percentage of children receiving free meals and the percentage bringing a packed lunch have increased, while the percentage buying a school meal or having other arrangements has decreased. The total number of meals provided by LEAs has remained more or less constant. The chart overleaf indicates the position for England.

The number of children receiving free meals in England has risen dramatically since 1991. In 1991, 821,400 children had free school meals, whereas in 1993 the figure was 1,141,300 – a rise of 319,900, or nearly 40 per cent.

A UNIVERSAL SERVICE?

Most authorities still claim a 'universal' meals service. Many respondent authorities made special reference (with, one cannot help feeling, a touch of pride) to the fact that hot meals – often cooked on the premises – were available in all their schools.

There are, however, a small number of authorities (eight in 1993) which have taken advantage of the 1980 Act to abandon a universal service in favour of a service to recipients of free meals only. This residual service tends to be 'sandwiches only'. Buckinghamshire was one of the first to abandon its meals service, save for packed lunches supplied to 'free meal' children.

Since the introduction of LMS, however, information has been much more difficult to obtain. An LEA might have adopted a residuary service but individual schools may have decided on a different strategy.

Figure 8.1: **School meal arrangements 1989–1993**

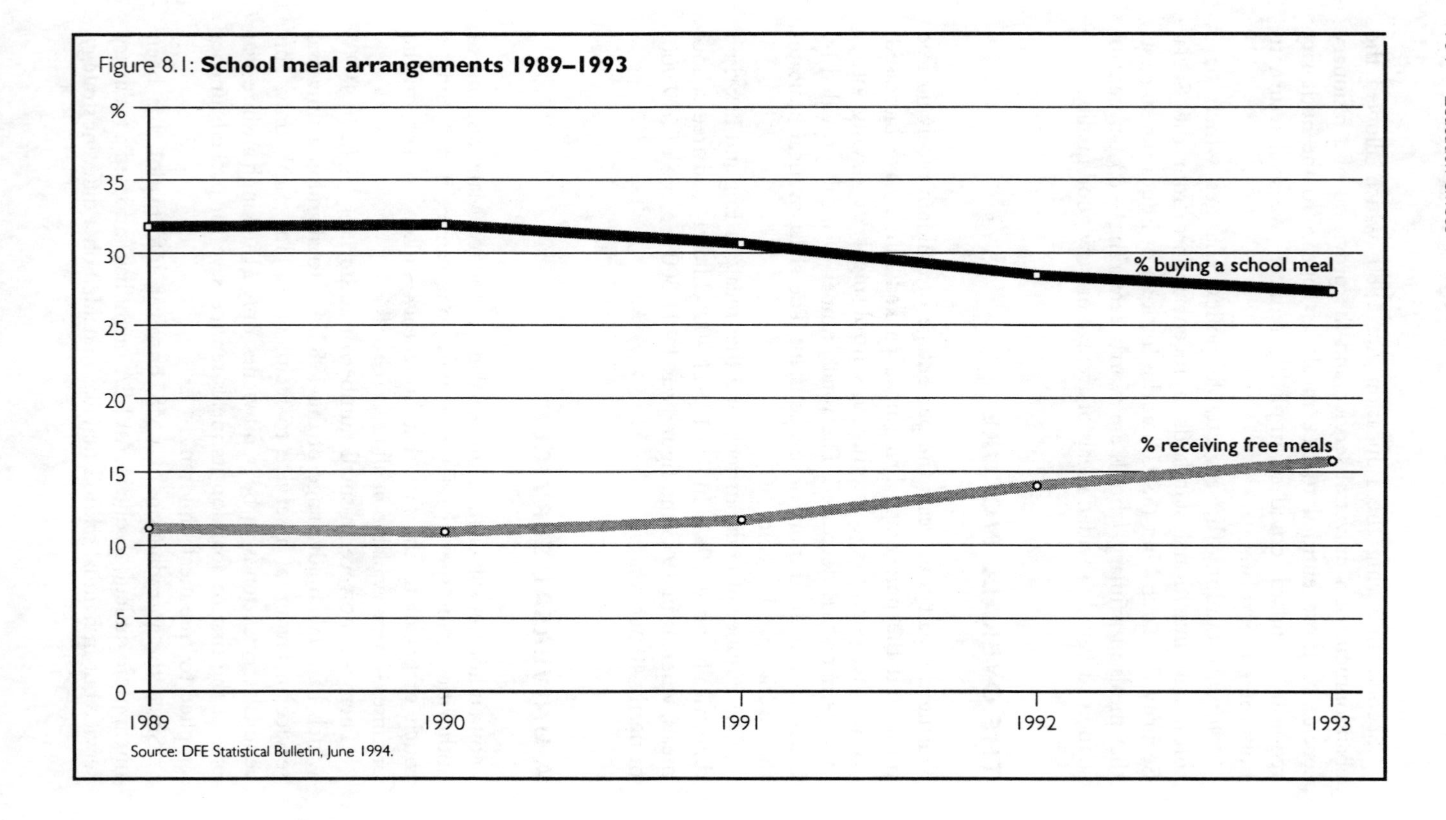

Source: DFE Statistical Bulletin, June 1994.

We know of at least one school in Buckinghamshire, for example, which has re-introduced a school meals service as a result of LMS.

HOW MUCH ARE MEALS?

Meal prices vary dramatically across authorities. The disparity reported by Berger in 1981 has continued throughout the decade. This was important in 1988 when family credit (former FIS) claimants ceased to be eligible to free meals and it was argued that compensation would be included in the benefit payment.

The introduction of LMS means that prices of meals can be determined at school rather than LEA level. However, in most authorities there is still an LEA-wide price. The table below shows the range of prices of meals in primary school dining centres in April 1993. We have selected the most expensive and the cheapest among London boroughs, metropolitan districts and English counties.

TABLE 8.1: **School meal prices in selected primary school dining centres in England April 1993**

	Borough/County	Price
London Boroughs	Hammersmith and Fulham	70p
	Kingston-upon-Thames	126p
Metropolitan Districts	Liverpool	70p
	Trafford	112p
English Counties	Humberside	55p
	Cambridgeshire	110p

Source: CIPFA, *Education Statistics, 1993-94 Estimates*

The table needs explanation. First, many schools/LEAs do not operate any or many dining centres – instead, if meals are provided as a general service they are provided in cash cafeterias which may or may not provide meals within the same price range. Second, where fixed price meals in dining centres are available, there may be some variation between schools in the LEA. The table, nevertheless, shows the disparity in the price of school meals. This difference is crucial for low-income families who are not in receipt of income support and therefore not entitled to free school meals. A low-income family in

Kingston-upon-Thames pays more than twice the school meal price it would in Humberside.

School meals – it depends on where you live

A single parent with two children under 10 has weekly earnings of £90 net of tax and NI. She receives child benefit of £18.10, one parent benefit of £6.05 and family credit of £49.30. This is a total net disposable income of £163.45. If she lived in Humberside, the bill for her children's school meals would be £5.50 a week or just over 10 per cent of her weekly family credit. If she lived in Kingston-upon-Thames she would face a bill of £12.60 – over 25 per cent of her family credit.

Many authorities seem to be continuing to provide the meals 'at cost' which often contains hidden subsidies. Local authorities are now, however – as a result of Compulsory Competitive Tendering – moving to an unsubsidised meals system:

> An unsubsidised meals service will be available in both the primary and secondary sectors from September 1993. Free school meals are provided via this provision.
>
> Outer London Borough

As authorities increase prices and reduce choice or ultimately abandon school meals services except for children entitled to free meals, children from low-income families not on income support will be further excluded.

TAKE UP

The take-up of free school meals is affected by two factors. First, there are those potentially eligible who have not registered their eligibility with the school/LEA. Second, there are those children authorised to take free school meals who do not, in fact, take them.

Data in respect of the first component is not available. In theory it should be possible to compare the numbers of school age children in families dependent on income support with data on children registered for free school meals. However, DSS statistics giving the age breakdown of dependent children are not readily available and it is therefore not possible to estimate take-up of registration.

Until 1993, LEAs were obliged to return information which they collected from schools to the DFE (DES) on numbers 'known to be eligible' for free meals on a specified day in January. This information was subsequently published through the DES statistical service. In January 1993, these data were collected directly from schools (as was information on prices of meals). This indicates the degree to which the 1988 devolution via LMS has occurred. Information collected in this direct way is not as complete as it was when collected through the LEAs and is no longer published. However, similar data collected by the Association of London Authorities from London boroughs for secondary schools in 1993 have been published.[11] This showed that across London 28.2 per cent of all pupils were authorised for free school meals. This average disguises wide variation. The following table shows the three boroughs with the highest registrations and the three with the lowest. Where known, the percentage of registered children actually taking school meals is shown.

TABLE 8.2: **Registration for and uptake of free school meals in selected London boroughs**

	% of pupils registered for free school meals in 1993	% of those authorised actually taking up the meals in 1993
Tower Hamlets	64.91	40.66
Hackney	56.1	–
Southwark	52.91	32.58
Havering	9.02	5.6
Sutton	8.7	–
Kingston	7.75	5.78

In our survey, we asked LEAs and schools to suggest reasons for both non-registration for free meals of eligible children and non-consumption of meals by children authorised to take free meals.

Of the LEAs who responded, 40 per cent stated that they had evidence that some parents on income support were not registering their children's entitlement. Many were reluctant to say how big a problem this was. However, some authorities we contacted had researched non-take-up and were able to come up with very precise estimates:

> 18.3 per cent of those eligible (1,465 pupils) were not taking free meals in January 1993.

> Approximately 30 per cent not taking meals – possibly friends take sandwiches or eat away.
>
> Anecdotal evidence from schools, hard to quantify. Likely to be (i) some children do not like school meals (ii) fear of stigma.
>
> Lower uptake in secondary sector – mainly due to commercial alternatives, peer pressure, etc.

A higher percentage of LEAs – 77 per cent – reported that a proportion of those authorised to take free meals were not, in fact, eating them. As we have indicated, this information is easier to quantify. The reasons given by LEAs for this were:

- A very small percentage state that they do not take the option of a free meal because of the way a particular school administers the scheme.
- Ignorance of the provision is likely to be the mean reason; dietary requirements may also be a factor.
- No statistics available. Reasons are preference for packed lunch, social stigma and dietary.
- Numbers eligible for free meals can be monitored against numbers taken; approximately 15 per cent not taken in 1993. Main reason – stigma of being identified as different from other pupils.
- Perhaps 18 per cent not taking up – some due to absence, some pupils bring packed lunches – often for religious/cultural reasons.
- 1. Some families only require free clothing but granted FSM automatically. 2. Peer group pressure. 3. Asian dietary requirements not sufficiently catered for. 4. Quality of food (particularly hot transported meals).

The fact that some children on income support were not taking meals which had been authorised should not be interpreted to mean that free meals were of little value to people on income support. Many parents we spoke to stressed the importance financially to them of free meals and indeed stressed the difficulties in the holidays when such meals were not available.

> *How come we don't get extra money when they're off school then? Cos I've got four children and that is a big boost. When they're on holiday, I'm spending about 20 to 30 pound extra on food and no one's helping me out through the holidays.*

TAKE-UP CAMPAIGNS

Some local authorities have gone to great lengths to promote take-up of school meals:

> A television campaign has been carried out, lasting six weeks in September 1992. A copy of the video of the publicity is available. Open evenings in schools were also arranged.

One metropolitan local authority provides

> an integrated benefit system (from Oct 1992) whereby completing one claim form results in automatic calculation of housing benefit/ council tax benefit and education benefits.

STIGMA

As CPAG has often asserted,[12] many LEAs and schools commented that stigma was one of the main reasons for low take-up of school meals. Children entitled to free meals are to a greater or lesser extent identifiable as 'different' and labelled with the stigma of poverty.

There are many ways at both LEA and school level in which this stigmatisation can be reduced or eliminated. In authorities such as Buckinghamshire, where there is effectively only a residuary school meals service, the identification of 'poor' children is inevitable – they alone will be in receipt of meals because there is a service only for such children.

In other areas we need to distinguish between meals provided in dining centres and meals provided in cash cafeterias. The former represents the traditional school meals service, with set meals provided at a fixed price and not paid for 'at the door'. The latter resembles the commercial cafeteria with a till for payment after food has been selected. Cash cafeterias are structurally more stigmatising than dining centres. Free meal children are not (in any case we could find) given cash to spend; rather, they are either given tokens or asked to identify themselves to the cashier who checks them on a list and allows them an 'authorised spend'. Since they will be in a queue with other 'cash paying' children, they are readily identifiable and thus open to stigmatisation. Theoretically, it would be possible to make cafeterias less stigmatising by issuing all children with tokens (some in exchange for cash, some identified as from a family on income support).

However, we were unable to identify any such schools.

The 'authorised spend' in cash cafeterias is usually based on the LEA price of a meal in a 'dining centre' and may not cover the cost of the meal the child wants, and so there is the possibility of double discrimination.[13] Several parents we spoke to commented:

> *My son came home from school and said 'I had my meal but I couldn't have my pudding mum'. The next day he came home and I said 'did you have your meal?' He said, 'I had two puddings today' ... I said 'yer what?'... He said 'I couldn't afford a meal and a pudding ... the pudding was really nice so I had enough for two puddings'... He's not allowed to have puddings no more. He's got to have a meal but ... the free school meal doesn't cover a meal...*

Although virtually unknown in 1979, cash cafeterias have become the norm in secondary schools and are beginning to make significant inroads in the primary school.

The cash cafeteria principle, even where run in a non-stigmatising way, can mean that the nutritional value of the school meal as described in the Black Report (see above) is negated. As one parent said:

> *At B— its ... a ... cafeteria sort of thing ... they have to go round and choose up ... to a pound a day ... You can't get a cooked meal at ... now it's just sandwiches or rolls or something like that. God knows what our Daniel spends his pound on! ... sweets I expect...*

This is exactly what the writers of the Black Report feared:

> It should be regarded as a matter of importance – on education and health grounds – to ensure that all children receive a school meal or adequate substitute ... To leave school children, especially young school children, to make their own free choices of what food is to be purchased would be wrong. Children will frequently prefer to consume foods high only in sugar and other sources of energy...[14]

Meals taken in traditional 'dining centres' are far from stigma-free. There may be discrimination at the point of collection of the dinner money if this is carried out overtly in class. In some schools there may be discrimination at the point of taking the meal, with 'free meal' children eating at different tables.[15]

The evidence in this chapter should make us question whether the education service continues to provide a 'welfare' function for children and families as envisaged by its architects. It is clear that the market forces now determining school meals make it more difficult to secure an adequate diet for children in low-income families and for schools to implement sound policies on nutrition and health. They signal the end of a universal service.

NOTES

1. N Berger, *The School Meals Service: from its beginning to the present day*, Northcourt House, 1990.
2. Education Act 1944 s49.
3. N Berger, *op cit*, p95.
4. CPAG, *Burying Beveridge: a detailed response to the Green Paper: Reform of Social Security*, CPAG, 1985, p63.
5. House of Commons Library Research Note No. 263, 2 November 1987, p7.
6. P Townsend and N Davidson (eds), *Inequalities in Health*, Penguin, 1982, p186.
7. *Ibid*, p187.
8. Department of Education and Science, *Nutrition in Schools*, DES, 1975.
9. But see, for example, Berger, *op cit.*
10. Social Science Research Unit, *Health in Primary Schools*, Institute of Education, 1994.
11. Association of Local Authorities (ALA), Press release dated 31 January 1994.
12. For example, L Bissett and J Coussins, *Badge of Poverty: a new look at the stigma attached to free school meals*, CPAG, 1982.
13. *Ibid*, p25.
14. P Townsend and N Davidson (eds), *op cit*, p186.
15. L Bissett and J Coussins, *op cit*, p21.

[illegible] adequate diet for children in low-income families or for teachers to implement [illegible] policies on nutrition and health. The [illegible] the end of universal school [illegible].

Notes

1. N. Dingwall, The Vanished Meal: School meals in Britain [illegible] to the present day, [illegible], 1990.
2. Education Act [illegible].
3. N. [illegible].
4. CPAG, [illegible] school [illegible] (CPAG [illegible]), Social [illegible] CPAG, 1985, p. [illegible].
5. [illegible] Commons [illegible] 2 November [illegible], p. [illegible].
6. [illegible] Townsend and N. [illegible] [illegible] Penguin [illegible].
7. ibid., p. [illegible].
8. Department of Education and Science, [illegible] Design [illegible].
9. But see, for example, [illegible].
10. School [illegible] Research [illegible] Primary School, Institute of Education, 19[illegible].
11. Association of [illegible] Authorities [illegible], press release dated [illegible] January 198[illegible].
12. For example, [illegible], [illegible] of [illegible] the [illegible] affected [illegible] CPAG, [illegible].
13. [illegible].
14. P. Townsend and N. Davidson (eds), [illegible], p. [illegible].
15. Robinson and [illegible], p. [illegible].

IV
Education divides

9 Social disadvantage and educational progress

The essential conditions to achieve excellence and fulfilment of talent – at whatever level – are those of diversity and choice.

Choice and Diversity, para 15.3

So far we have examined the impact of the avalanche of educational change since the late 1980s on educational *provision* – on the distribution of resources, on access and choice and on the costs of education for families. Our clear conclusion is of an increasingly fragmented and divided service, with a strong shift away from the idea of a national education service. In one sense this is in line with the aim of government policy, to create greater diversity of *institutional* provision, with the national curriculum and its assessment providing the common linking threads. But as we have seen, this diversity can too often be translated into divisions and inequalities in provision.

Yet this diversity *could* be justified if the results and outcomes from education were becoming *more equal* as a result of recent educational changes; if this growing diversity were – contrary to expectations – leading to fairer chances for children from different social backgrounds, particularly those from socially disadvantaged areas. Certainly supporters of the current reforms have come close to claiming that the national curriculum, financial devolution to schools and greater parental choice will *by themselves* bring about just this shift to more equal opportunities for all children. It is to this crucial question that we now turn. Inevitably our coverage is on the more measurable outcomes, such as assessment and examination data.

EDUCATIONAL PERFORMANCE AND SOCIAL INEQUALITY

As we saw in Chapter 3, the British educational system has long been marked by sharp inequalities in educational outcomes for different social groups. Educational reforms in the 1960s – for example, the move to comprehensive secondary education and developments in primary education following the Plowden Report – attempted to reduce some of these inequalities *within* the system. In the 1980s, one of the driving forces behind educational reform was the belief that overall standards of education in Britain were lagging behind many other industrial countries. This shortfall was in terms of both:

- absolute levels of performance, for example, as measured by international tests or other assessment data, *and*
- persistence in education beyond the minimum school leaving age and into higher education.

It was widely agreed that a prime reason for overall low standards lay not in performance at the *top* of the range but in performance in the *lower* half of the distribution. International comparisons suggested that Britain, or more often England and Wales, was distinguished by a long tail of low performance. Thus, in the 1980s international science performance tables at age 10+, 61 per cent of the schools in the English sample had average scores of less than those of the *lowest* school in Japan.[1] Japan – the highest scoring country – owed its high position in significant part to a compact distribution of results – that is, the Japanese system had very successfully raised the performance of its lower performing schools and pupils, thereby effectively raising its national score.

Other countries, such as the US, which have consistently done poorly in these international assessments, regularly scoring below Britain even on assessments based on American standard tests, have also been marked by a long tail of low performance. It is no coincidence that in the US there are enormous inequalities in education between different social and ethnic groups.[2] And again, it is no coincidence that in trying to raise its international position in line with the national 'US Goals 2000' programme (Goal 4 is to make American children 'first in the world in mathematics and science achievement' by the year 2000), many programmes are now targeted at the most disadvantaged groups.

GENDER, RACE AND SOCIAL CLASS

Over the past 20 years, inequalities in educational performance have been analysed in terms of gender, race and social class. In this study we have concentrated on the social dimension, particularly for the most disadvantaged and poorest groups. But first, we briefly summarise some recent data on educational performance by gender and race.

Recent data clearly indicate that many of the inequalities in educational performance between boys and girls have been either very substantially reduced or even reversed. While girls traditionally did better at younger ages in many educational tests, which was sometimes attributed to more rapid rates of maturation, this advantage faded at higher and more selective levels. But this trend has changed rapidly with higher rates of entry to examinations by girls and less 'cooling out' by the system. Girls, on average, achieved about the same proportion of 5+ higher grade GCE/CSE as boys at the beginning of the 1980s. But by 1992/93, 46 per cent of girls achieved 5+ GCSE (A-C), as against 37 per cent of boys. By then girls were more likely to stay on at school beyond the minimum age and a higher proportion (35 per cent as against 31 per cent) were entering A/AS level in 1992/93 at age 17, although boys achieved a marginally higher average pass rate.

In 1992, for the first time, there were proportionately more young women *entering* higher education than young men. Unemployment among female graduates was substantially lower than that for their male counterparts.[3] There were, of course, many remaining inequalities – in terms of subjects studied and the prestige of higher education institutions attended – as well as many inequalities in treatment. However, on gender grounds, perhaps the greatest cause for concern in the mid-1990s should be the minimum age male school-leaver from disadvantaged areas, who was much more likely to leave school without qualifications than girls in the same area.

Given the many different ethnic minority groups, their different lengths of settlement in this country and their scattered location, this is a much more difficult area to summarise. A useful starting point is the Swann Committee[4] in 1985, which reviewed educational performance by ethnic minority groups. This confirmed the pattern of 'under achievement' by pupils of Afro-Caribbean origin, though there was some evidence of relative improvement in examination results over the period studied by the Committee (1978-1982).

For other groups, the pattern was quite varied. Asians as a group often tended to do as well as the white population, but there was evidence that this concealed many differences. Thus, Bangladeshi pupils tended to perform less well than many other groups. The reasons for these patterns were complex and involved social, cultural and educational factors.

But the picture has changed since 1985. Some studies continue to show that children from certain ethnic minorities perform less well on average in the early and middle stages of education[5] than the 'white' group of pupils. But the gap is closing over the final stages of compulsory education, at least on the basis of examination results. Indeed, many ethnic groups now significantly outperform their white peers *in the same area* at the latter stages of compulsory education. And recent Association of Metropolitan Authorities (AMA) data in terms of progress made during secondary schooling up to GCSE, suggest that the *poorest* rate of progress is made by those classified as white.[6] Thus, from a lower starting point ethnic minority pupils appear to be 'catching up', particularly in the later stages of their school careers. It may be that these ability measures at an earlier point understate the capacity of pupils from ethnic minority backgrounds, or it may be that higher motivation, better attitudes to schooling and in some cases better attendance rates by ethnic minority pupils all help to translate this more effectively into examination performance at the end of compulsory schooling.

Studies at the post-compulsory phase indicate that ethnic minority groups tend to end up with higher overall levels of qualification than equivalent white groups from the same area as a result of their increased persistence in education.[7] Smith and Tomlinson found that in the post-compulsory phase, both Asians and West Indians were 'substantially more likely than white people to pursue further study, both full-time and part-time, after leaving school'. Recent figures, for 1990 and 1991, show that ethnic minorities have considerably increased their representation in higher education – particularly in the 'new universities' – but there are still significant differences between groups, between institutions and between subjects.[8]

This changing pattern suggests grounds for optimism. Nonetheless, it is important to sound some notes of caution. First, despite the improved qualification levels among ethnic groups, research studies continue to show evidence of discrimination in the labour market against ethnic minority youngsters.[9] Some studies suggest that part of the motivation for increased education beyond the compulsory level may be discrimination in the job market. Secondly, we must not forget the benchmark of comparison: it may be that the comparative white population in many inner city areas is itself becoming *more* disadvantaged and therefore its educational performance is in relative decline. Finally, it may be that this economic and social disadvantage, shared by many ethnic minority groups and by some white groups, is increasingly the key factor affecting educational achievement.

EDUCATIONAL CHANGE AND SOCIAL INEQUALITY: SOME RECENT TRENDS

The educational system in Britain in the late 1980s and the first half of the 1990s experienced a very rapid expansion, judged against its previous sluggish performance, in terms of qualifications obtained, staying-on rates beyond 16 and entry to higher education, to take three commonly used measures. The proportions of the age group in England obtaining 5+ higher grade (A-C) GCSE increased from about 26 per cent in 1987/88 to 41 per cent in 1993; the proportion of 16 year olds in full-time education rose from 49 per cent in 1987/88 to 73 per cent in 1993/94; and in higher education the 'age participation index' doubled from 13 per cent in 1981 to 27.8 per cent in 1992.

While these increases coincided with a spate of educational policy changes in the late 1980s, these reforms could have made only a minor contribution. First, the increase in qualifications and staying-on rate followed the introduction of the GCSE in 1988, well before the 1988 Education Reform Act came into effect. Second, the changes were most marked in those parts of the system which were initially least affected by the curriculum reforms; for example, at 14-plus and 16-plus. Finally, there were other major changes – in numbers in the age group leaving school, in labour market conditions and loss of entitlement to benefit for those aged 16-17 – which all influenced these outcomes.[10] While the credit for this increase should go primarily to those most directly involved – the young people themselves, their teachers and schools – it would be churlish to deny some role to recent policy developments, if only because the reforms concentrated attention on educational performance, particularly that measured by external examination results.

However, we need to ask two further questions. First, what is the position for younger age groups, where recent policy changes would have had a greater impact? And second, have the increases in qualifications and staying-on rates at higher levels resulted in greater equality of outcomes for different social groups? Inevitably the data available is patchy; there is only limited trend data, much of this at a high level of aggregation.

PRIMARY LEVEL

In principle, national curriculum assessment data in the form of Standard Assessment Tasks (SATs) should provide the best information on trends. But substantial changes in assessment procedures and coverage, and the boycott by the main teacher unions of some of the SAT assessment procedures in 1993, mean that there is little usable trend data. However, analysis of the 1991 and 1992 SAT data for seven year olds shows a clear relationship at an LEA level with the social class of households with children under 16. Analysing data from 107 LEAs, McCallum found that:

> between one-quarter and one-half of the differences (variance) in SAT performance of seven year old pupils in different LEAs is associated with the differences in the proportion of households with heads in social class I and II. The differences between LEAs in the top and bottom 10 per cent in terms of the proportions in social class I and II correspond to a difference in DES rankings of well over 50 (out of a total of 107 LEAs).[11]

Figure 9.1, based on data from the 1992 SAT results on the reading component at Key Stage 1 for LEAs in England, shows the clear relationship between the proportions of children from partly skilled and unskilled manual households and the proportions of pupils getting Level 2 (the expected level) or above. This shows that even criterion-referenced data such as SATs are still heavily influenced by social factors.

This data could be criticised for its high level of aggregation. However, other studies relying on school level data suggest that social factors have a strong influence. The Leeds University evaluation of the 1992 Key Stage 1 SAT data,[12] based on 89 schools in 52 different LEAs, found a number of significant differences between groups of children in their sample. In addition to gender (girls generally did better than boys) and season of birth (winter-born children did consistently better; summer-born worse), there were marked differences between children from different neighbourhoods. Thus, more than

Figure 9.1: **1992 SAT at KS1 – percentage of pupils at Level 2 or above**

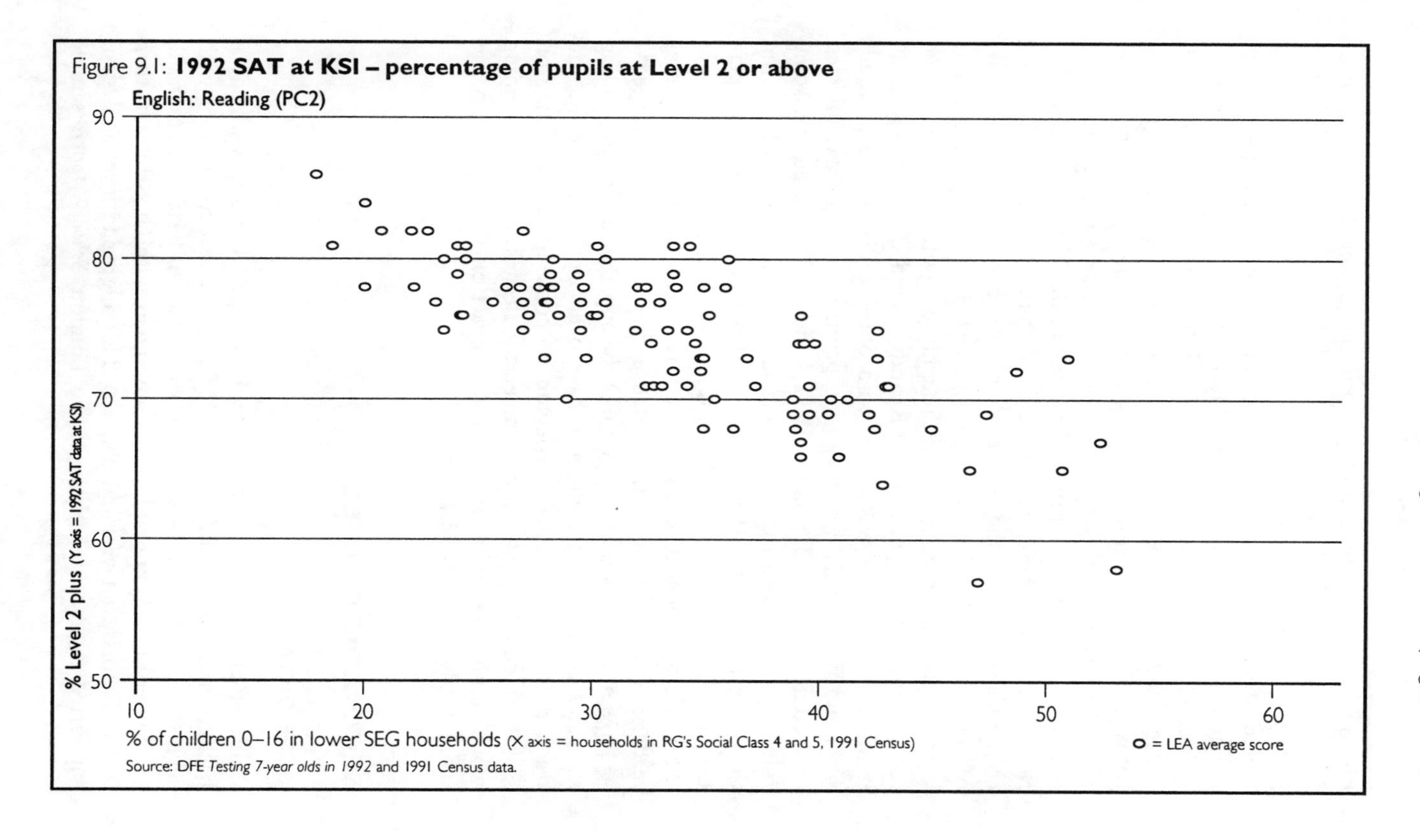

Source: DFE *Testing 7-year olds in 1992* and 1991 Census data.

one-quarter of children from low-status neighbourhoods scored at or below Level 1 and 10 per cent at Level 3 or above in English. The pattern was reversed for those from high-status areas: 27 per cent scored at Level 3 or above, 10 per cent at Level 1 or below. The differences were even more marked in maths, but less so in science.

These studies underline the continuing importance of social background factors in influencing performance levels. Has the gap between top and bottom scoring groups actually grown over time? Here the evidence is much more scanty (not least because there are few consistent data over time). The study of the National Foundation for Educational Research (NFER), *Reading in Recession*, which compared results from the same reading test applied to national samples of pupils in 1987 and again in 1991, reported a decline of 2.5 points between the two testing periods, roughly equivalent to about three months in reading age. While this study included a relatively small number of schools, it was in line with other studies at this period.[13] Cato and Whetton (1991), reviewing primary reading data collected by 26 different LEAs during the 1980s, concluded that there was some evidence of decline in reading scores in 19 LEAs, particularly during the latter part of the 1980s. Work by Lake based on reading performance of all seven/eight year olds in Buckinghamshire throughout the 1980s concludes that this decline was concentrated among poorer readers; he links this explicitly to increased economic disadvantage.[14]

However, other studies suggest that the apparent decline in reading standards at age seven/eight may have been caused by pressure on teachers from the national curriculum to concentrate more time on science, technology and other subjects.[15] Less attention to reading would almost certainly have had most impact on weaker readers and more disadvantaged pupils.

SECONDARY LEVEL

GCSE DATA

Achievement at 16-plus also shows a strong relationship with social background. Data at LEA level for 1992[16] show that correlations with such social background variables as social class of head of household, car ownership and unemployment are higher with GCSE results than for SATs for seven-year-old children. This aggregate level analysis is supported by recent analysis of the London *School Matters* sample during the secondary phase. Commenting on the GCSE results at the end of the 1980s, Sammons concludes that 'social class remains a very important predictor of later academic achievement and ... the gap in attainment between non-manual and other social class groups increased steadily throughout their school careers'.[17]

Trend data on GCSE results at the LEA level since 1988 throws further light on the pattern of increase in different areas. In Figure 9.2 (overleaf) LEAs (excluding those in Inner London) have been grouped into three categories: the most disadvantaged (25 per cent with the highest proportion of children from semi or unskilled manual backgrounds), the most advantaged (25 per cent with the highest proportion of children from professional and higher non-manual backgrounds) and the remaining 50 per cent. Examining the proportions of children obtaining GCSE 5+ higher grades shows a clear pattern. All three areas increase more or less at a similar percentage rate of gain (approximately 50 per cent more between 1988 and 1993). But this means that the *actual rate* diverges, with the more advantaged areas ending up *further* ahead. To close the gap, poorer areas would have to gain at a *significantly* higher rate.

STAYING ON RATES

The numbers of young people aged 16 and 17 staying on in education at school and in college in England beyond the minimum school leaving age have increased sharply over the last few years to 78 per cent of 16 year olds and 64 per cent of 17 year olds in 1992/93.[18] There is considerable variation between authorities. Some have twice as many 16 and 17 year olds in full-time education. In 1992/93, full-time participation at age 16 ranged from about 50 per cent to 85 per cent, and at age 17 from about 35 per cent to 70 per cent.

In 1992/93, Barnet, for example, had 87 per cent of its 16 year olds and 71 per cent of its 17 year olds in full-time education, while Knowsley had only 49 per cent of its 16 year olds and 33 per cent of its 17 year olds. Generally there is a north/south divide, but with 'pockets of variation': Newham, one of the outer London boroughs, had a relatively low participation rate, while Sefton, Stockport, Bury, North Tyneside and Newcastle – all metropolitan districts – had relatively high rates. There is a clear north/south divide if we consider the list of authorities with the highest rates – Richmond, Sutton, Hertfordshire and Barnet – and the lowest – Knowsley, Salford, Sunderland and Sandwell. Overall, Greater London and the south-east had higher full-time

Figure 9.2: **Percentage of age group obtaining 5+ GCSE 1988–1994 by LEA type**

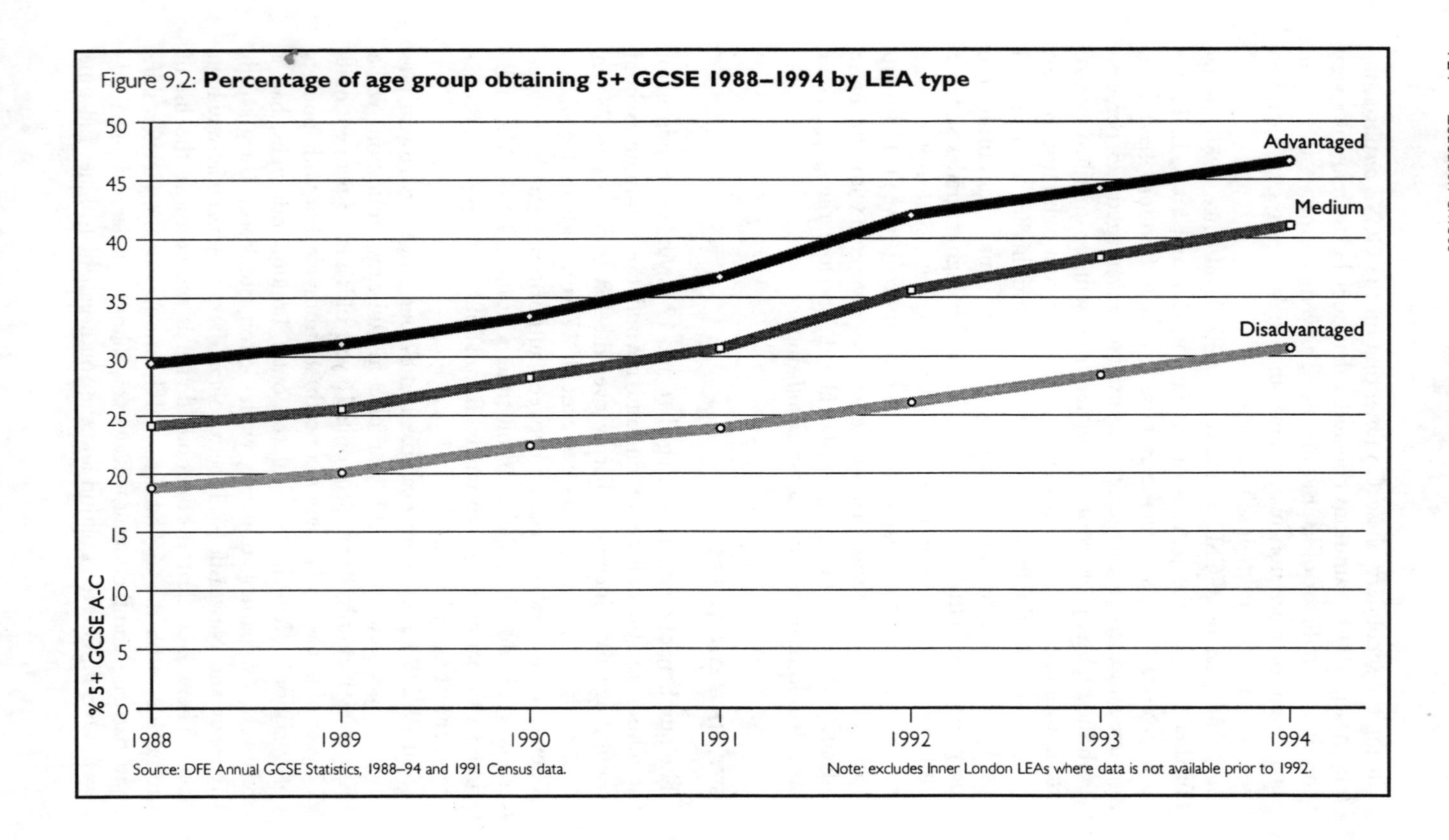

Source: DFE Annual GCSE Statistics, 1988–94 and 1991 Census data.

Note: excludes Inner London LEAs where data is not available prior to 1992.

participation rates and lower part-time rates than other regions, while the north had the lowest full-time rate and the lowest rate overall.

Figure 9.3 (overleaf) shows the overall for proportions of the age group still in full-time education at age 17 between 1988 and 1993 for LEAs grouped into the most advantaged and disadvantaged in social class terms. This shows the same pattern of divergence as in the GCSE results, though this time it is rather less marked. As we showed in Chapter 4, LEAs with higher staying-on rates receive additional central government funding on a *pro rata* basis. The effect may well be to ensure more attractive and varied post-16 provision than is possible in LEAs which are trapped in a vicious circle of low staying-on rates.

WHO STAYS ON?

Who are the young people most likely to be staying on in education, and why do they do so? The answer is those who already have higher educational qualifications at age 16 who come from non-manual and well-educated backgrounds.[19] The reasons for staying on are clear: better qualifications and the chance of a better job in due course; the process of securing qualifications with some 'market value' and converting them into employment opportunities. It is also clear that those least likely to stay on are those *most* in need of this boost: those from poorer families which themselves have the least education.

This social difference provides the best explanation for the difference in staying-on rates between local authorities. We can see that young people from different social backgrounds follow different routes from school into work or unemployment. Young people from manual backgrounds are much less likely to pursue routes through full-time education, especially if it involves A-level study.[20]

Other factors are also at work. It seems likely that young people are more likely to stay on in authorities where the pupil population *as a whole* comes from more advantaged backgrounds. The local labour market may also be an important factor. Poor or no qualifications increase the risk of chronic unemployment.[21] The changes in the benefit regulations introduced in 1988 which removed entitlement from 16 and 17 year olds and instead offered a Youth Training Scheme (YTS) place have also had some impact on staying-on rates.

Studies of successive groups of school leavers show that those most likely to have been affected by the withdrawal of benefit were young people with no examination passes, from manual homes, living in

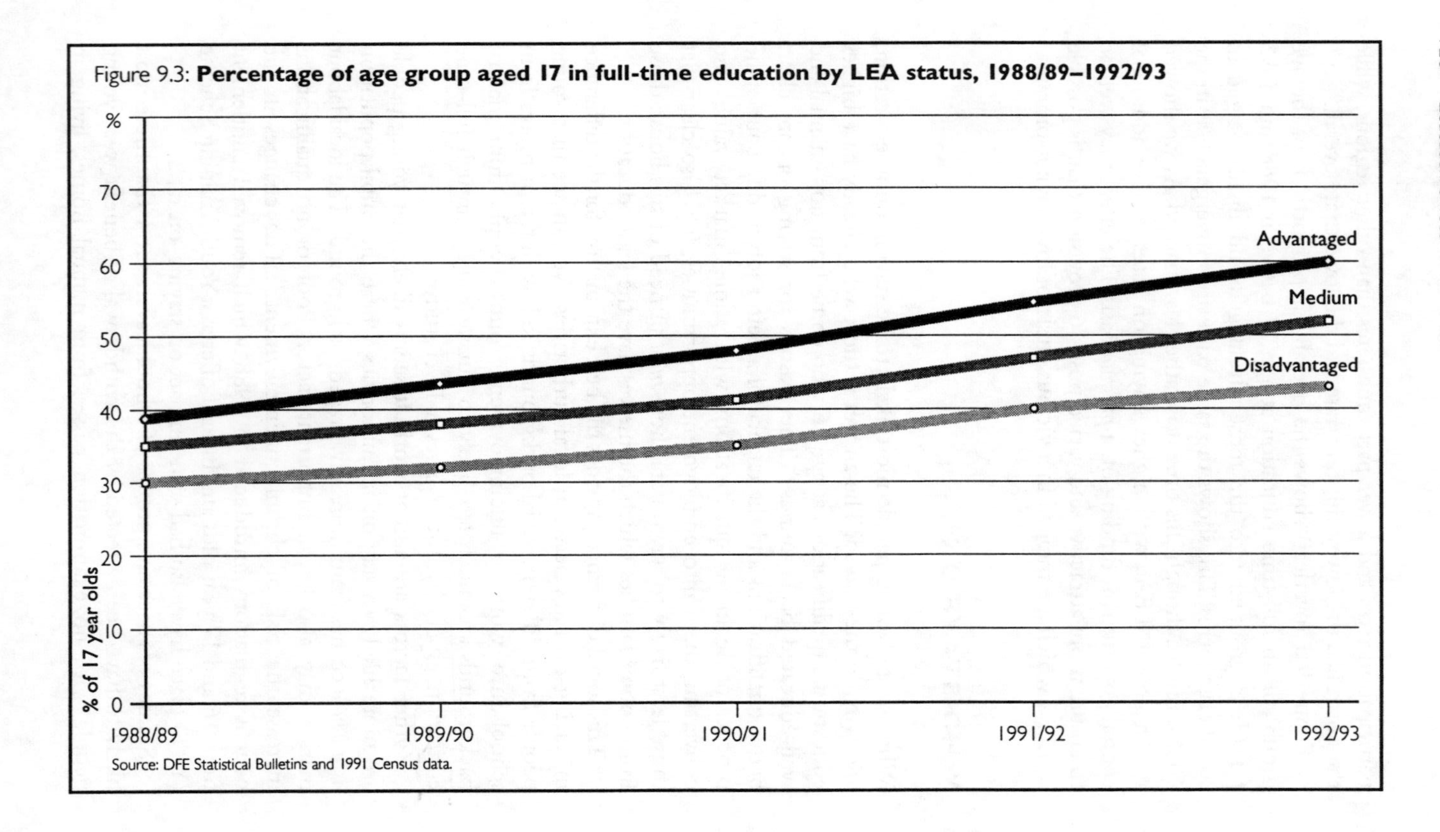

Figure 9.3: **Percentage of age group aged 17 in full-time education by LEA status, 1988/89–1992/93**

Source: DFE Statistical Bulletins and 1991 Census data.

areas of mid-to-high unemployment.[22] By 1988 there had been a decrease in the number of young people who were unemployed and a corresponding increase in the numbers taking up a YTS place. However, those who refused the offer of a YTS place shared the characteristics of those originally most likely to be out of work and also included young mothers and individuals with a disability which limited the type of conditions and environment in which they could work.

The numbers of individuals with characteristics next most likely to make them 'at risk' of unemployment[23] were affected rather differently by the changes in benefit regulations. While the numbers obtaining full-time employment increased, those taking up places on YTS schemes decreased and the numbers staying on in full-time education also increased. Overall, however, 'the educational participation rates of that quarter of young people who were most "at risk" of being out of work had previously been low and remained so'.[24]

Table 9.1 shows the destinations of the two cohorts of young people 'at risk' of being out of work following changes in the benefit system.

TABLE 9.1: **Destination of young people 'at risk' of being out of work following changes in the benefit system**

	Full-time education %	Full-time job %	YTS %	Out of work %	Other %
(Pre-benefit changes)					
• most at risk	4	25	42	21	9
• next most at risk	11	29	42	11	7
(Post-benefit changes)					
• most at risk	5	22	52	9	12
• next most at risk	15	34	38	6	7

Source: *YCS No 20*, 1993

Additionally, while youth trainees were guaranteed a place on a YTS, in reality many young people in particular parts of the country had to wait for long periods of time before being taken on, and most of the government youth training schemes mirrored the segregation by race and gender that is found in the external labour market.

The type and mix of post-16 provision on offer is also important to staying-on rates. For example, in 1987, six out of ten young people staying on in education came from a 'high' social background. But only 17 per cent were intending to go to FE college, while 46 per cent intended to stay on at school. Only three out of ten came from 'manual' backgrounds; but in this group almost the same proportion were intending to go to college or stay on at school.[25] Not surprisingly, young people moving on to FE college for their post-16 education were considerably more sceptical about the value of what their school had offered them.

Young people in the inner city

Young people from schools in disadvantaged neighbourhoods in the inner city, compared with young people from less disadvantaged neighbourhoods:

- were less likely at 16-plus to stay on in education
- were more likely to be out of work
- were more likely to leave at Easter of their last year, without waiting to take any exams
- yet were just as positive about their school experience: neither group condemned school as 'a waste of time', and more than half in both groups thought that school had given them 'more confidence', been a 'preparation for life' and taught them 'things that would be useful in a job'.

Gray, Jesson and Sime, *Education and Training Opportunities in the Inner City*, 1991

The youth service also plays a crucial role for young people, particularly those most likely to drop out of mainstream schooling and those with acute social needs such as homelessness and unemployment.[26] Yet youth work budgets have suffered from major cuts. The Community and Youth Workers Union estimated that between 1979 and 1983 there were 12.3 per cent cuts in real terms across the country which have never been restored,[27] while since 1990 the removal of an identified element for the Youth Service in central government funding for local authorities and the threat of 'capping' have targeted non-statutory expenditure. And this pressure has increased. Sixty-two per cent of the local authorities surveyed by the National Youth Agency in 1993 reported reduced expenditure on the Youth Service (in some cases 20 per cent or more), compared with 14 per cent reporting growth and 24 per cent a 'standstill'. This compared with 1992 when only 39 per cent reported reductions; 19 per cent were still increasing their budgets and 42 per cent stayed where they were.[28]

There are also serious questions to ask about the group of 16 and 17 year olds who drop out of both education, training and work – the numbers who go 'missing'.[29] Estimates for 1992 suggest that there were 97,300 16 and 17 year olds not in full-time education and without jobs or Youth Training places, who were not receiving any form of benefit. These young people are likely to be those at the bottom of the educational ladder – those who leave school without taking any exams, at the earliest possible opportunity, with least chances in an increasingly competitive job market: 'These young people do not figure in official statistics. There is no evidence that they are not in need, as no research into this group has been carried out. There is reason to be extremely concerned about them.'[30]

Final conclusions about the long-term impact of the series of educational reforms in the late 1980s and early 1990s must wait for more detailed analysis. However, the interim conclusion from data available so far must be that the inequalities in educational performance which galvanised some of the educational reforms in the 1960s are still, in the mid-1990s, as sharp as ever. Moves to lay down a common national curriculum framework and to encourage greater diversity of provision appear to have made little, if any, impact on these inequalities. Indeed, if anything, the evidence suggests that these inequalities may actually have increased at the secondary and post-secondary levels, in a context of overall rising levels of qualification and staying-on rates. It is impossible at this point to say whether this divergence is the result of increased social and economic polarisation or of the educational changes themselves.

NOTES

1. N Postlethwaite, *Science Achievement in Seventeen Countries*, Pergamon Press, 1988.
2. See J Kozol, *Savage Inequalities: children in America's schools*, Harper Perennial, 1991.
3. Department for Education, *Statistical Bulletin, 26/93: Women in Post-Compulsory Education*, 1993.
4. Department of Education and Science, *Education For All: the report of a committee of inquiry into the education of children from ethnic minority groups*, Cmnd 9453, Swann Committee, HMSO, 1985.

5. A F Osborn and N Butler, *Ethnic Minority Children: a comparative study from birth to five years*, CRE, 1985; ILEA, *The Junior School Project, Part A and Part C*, ILEA, 1986; D J Smith and S Tomlinson, *The School Effect: a study of multi-racial comprehensives*, Policy Studies Institute, 1989.
6. S Thomas quoted in P Sammons, 'Gender, ethnic and socio-economic differences in attainment and progress: a longitudinal analysis of student achievement over nine years', *British Educational Research Journal*, 21(4), 1994.
7. B Tizard et al, *Young Children at School in the Inner City*, Lawrence Erlbaum, 1988.
8. T Modood, 'The number of ethnic minority students in British higher education: some grounds for optimism', *Oxford Review of Education*, 19(2), 1993, pp167-82.
9. J Eggleston, D Dunn and M Anjali, *Education For Some: the educational and vocational experiences of 15-18 year old members of ethnic minority groups*, Trentham Books, 1986.
10. See J Gray, D Jesson and M Tranmer, *Boosting Post-16 Participation in Full-Time Education: a study of some key factors*, Youth Cohort Study 20, Employment Department, Sheffield, 1993, for an analysis of some of these factors.
11. I McCallum, 'Testing seven year olds – performance and context', *Projecting School Rolls and Assessing Performance*, London Research Centre, 1993, p22.
12. National Union of Teachers and University of Leeds, *Testing and Assessing Six and Seven Year Olds: the evaluation of the 1992 Key Stage 1 National Curriculum assessment*, NUT, 1993.
13. T Gorman and C Fernandez, *Reading in Recession*, NFER, 1992.
14. M Lake, 'Surveying all the factors', *Language and Learning*, June 1991.
15. R J Campbell and S R Neill, *Four Years On: the failure of curriculum reform at Key Stage 1*, University of Warwick, November 1993.
16. I McCallum, *op cit.*
17. P Sammons, *op cit.*
18. Department for Education, *Statistical Bulletin 11/94*, DFE, August 1994.
19. Gray, Jesson and Tranmer, *op cit*, Table 2.1, p20.
20. N Sime, C Pattie and J Gray, *What Now? The transition from school to the labour market amongst 16 to 19 year olds, England and Wales Youth Cohort Study*, Research and Development No. 62, Youth Cohort Series No. 14, Sheffield University Division of Education, 1990.
21. K Roberts and C Chadwick, *Transitions into the Labour Market: the new routes of the 1980s. A study of transitions 1984-87*, Research and Development No. 65, Youth Cohort Series No. 16, Sheffield University Division of Education, 1991.
22. *Ibid*, p4.
23. While the group most at risk comprised individuals with no graded

examination passes, from manual backgrounds, living in areas of quite high unemployment, this second cohort was less disadvantaged with regard to at least one of the above conditions.

24. Gray, Jesson and Tranmer, *op cit.*
25. D Jesson, J Gray and N Sime, *Participation, Progress and Performance in Post-Compulsory Education. England and Wales Youth Cohort Study*, Research and Development No. 64, Youth Cohort Series No. 15, Sheffield University Division of Education, 1991, p5ff.
26. See Her Majesty's Inspectorate, *Responsive Youth Work: the Youth Service and urgent social needs*, HMSO, 1990; and *Effective Youth Work in Clubs and Projects*, HMSO, 1993.
27. Community and Youth Workers Union, *Youth Work and Community Work into the 21st Century: policy statement*, CYWU, 1992.
28. Figures from National Youth Agency, *Policy Updates*, April and June 1993.
29. D Istance, G Rees and H Williamson, *Young People Not in Education, Training or Employment in South Glamorgan*, South Glamorgan Training and Enterprise Council, 1994.
30. I Maclagan, *Four Years' Severe Hardship: young people and the benefits gap*, Youthaid/COYPSS/Barnardos, 1993. Quoted in Istance, Rees and Williamson, *op cit*, p9. See also *Working Brief*, July 1994, issue 56, pp12-13.

10 Conclusion: diversity or division?

'I am not prepared to see children in some parts of this country having to settle for a second-class education,' wrote John Major in his foreword to *Choice and Diversity: a new framework for schools*.[1] We set out to examine this claim, particularly for children growing up in poor families in the 1980s and 1990s. Here we summarise our findings chapter by chapter.

SUMMARY

EDUCATIONAL POLICY AND POOR PEOPLE

The very real backdrop is the sharply widening gap in income between rich and poor since the early 1980s, despite an overall rise in income and wealth. Families with dependent children now form an increasingly large proportion of the poorest ten per cent of households, and they are often concentrated in disadvantaged urban areas. In education, the proportions of pupils at national level obtaining qualifications, staying on at school and entering higher education rose sharply in the late 1980s and 1990s. But, as with economic growth, overall improvement does not mean that all groups share equally in these gains. Is there a growing educational divide mirroring these social and economic divisions? And what are the effects of the spate of educational reforms on educational opportunities for children from poor families? These are the questions we set out to answer. (Chapter 1)

From the outset, schooling has been about more than the 'three Rs'. Educational policy has always had underlying social objectives, even though the focus of this social dimension has shifted. At the start the concern was to get children from poor families into the classroom; later, school meals and school-based health services were to help children 'take full advantage of the education provided for them'. The second stage focused on equality of educational opportunity: comprehensive secondary reorganisation in the late 1960s set out to ensure equal access to educational opportunities for all children. But equality of *access* did not necessarily lead to greater equality of *result*. The third stage focused on raising educational quality and performance in the poorest areas. In the fourth stage in the 1980s and 1990s, this 'social dimension' to educational policy has been explicitly rejected as 'social engineering'. In its place the emphasis is now on individual choice and opportunity in the educational market place, with the national curriculum providing the common framework; and pupil assessment, league tables and school inspection reports the 'market intelligence' on relative quality. The onus for success is now placed firmly on *individual* pupils (or their parents), or on individual schools. (Chapter 2)

This emphasis on the educational market and the explicit rejection of a social dimension in educational policy meant that by the late 1980s, in a new form of political correctness, the links between educational performance and social and economic conditions had become almost a taboo subject in public policy debate. And yet ignoring the problem has not meant that it has gone away. Evidence continues to accumulate that the relative gap in educational opportunities and results for children from different social backgrounds is as wide as ever. Data for urban areas in 1993 show that, in the poorest districts, comprehensive school pupils achieve on average approximately half the success rate in getting 5+ higher grade GCSEs of comprehensive pupils in the most advantaged urban areas. This does not mean that individual children from the poorest circumstances cannot succeed. But the chances are heavily stacked against them. The reasons lie in a combination of social and environmental conditions, family circumstances – including low income and poverty – poor educational opportunities and ineffective schools. (Chapter 3)

THE NEW MARKET SYSTEM

Much recent debate on standards and quality in education has been divorced from questions of resources and funding, as if these made no difference. But these questions are now rightly returning to the centre of debate. Overall expenditure on schools has grown only marginally since the 1970s; capital and maintenance expenditure fell and stayed very low, seen in the very poor state of many school buildings in the 1990s. Per pupil expenditure rose as numbers of pupils fell in the 1980s, but has now begun to fall back sharply, particularly at secondary level. Central government allocation to local education authorities includes a weighting for social needs, but this has been significantly reduced since April 1994, and the criteria used sometimes allocate more to some local authorities with apparently lower levels of need. LEAs overall take only limited account of social factors in allocating resources to schools. The result is that in many areas schools in disadvantaged areas receive only very limited additional funding. Many other sources of funding, such as the Urban Programme and Section 11 funding for ethnic minorities, have been cut back or phased out. Schools must increasingly resort to raising their own funds. The overall funding picture is one of anomalies between areas and schools, which are hard to understand and even harder to justify, when some schools have increasingly greater command over resources, while others decline. (Chapter 4)

Increased parental choice lies at the centre of the educational market. 'Open enrolment', greater diversity through 'opted out' grant maintained schools and City Technology Colleges, schemes such as 'assisted places' in fee-paying schools, and new opportunities for schools to specialise and select pupils with particular skills, might all in principle be thought to increase choice and diversity for pupils and their parents. But in practice increased choice for a minority reduces choice for others. Choice depends significantly on where you live; the most popular schools are increasingly able to select their intake, rather than the other way round. The 'flip-side' is the rejected 'sink' school with declining numbers and resources, often located in a disadvantaged area. A further consequence of increased autonomy for schools is the steep growth in the number of children excluded from school. There are now potentially thousands of such 'unwanted' and disaffected children excluded from any form of schooling, many in inner city and other poor areas. (Chapter 5)

Access to pre-school provision also depends very heavily on where you live and on local authority policy. Some local authorities provide nursery education explicitly as a way of reducing the effects of poverty and boosting the chances of disadvantaged children. But others make very little or no provision. Nursery education is widely supported in theory but patchy in practice. Much daycare for working parents is restricted to better-off and well-educated parents' private arrangements. (Chapter 6)

THE REAL COSTS OF EDUCATION

Access to education for children from poor families is restricted if children cannot be properly clothed or equipped for school. If free school meals are stigmatising children will not eat them and will therefore lack the nourishment to get the best from the education provided. Although most LEAs still give clothing grants, there is considerable geographical variation in criteria for eligibility and amount. Overall amounts have not increased in the past three years, remaining around £34 per award. Awards are usually available only when changing schools rather than on an annual basis. School second-hand clothing clubs are on the increase, and charities are used to bridge the gap. The cost of getting to school for those living nearer than the statutory two or three miles is increasing, and with more traffic on the roads parents do not wish their children to cycle or walk. Very few LEAs provide comprehensive support for children from poor families. Thus the financial burden on poor parents increases. School charging policies were found to vary enormously between authorities, and 'voluntary' contributions were often felt by parents to be 'obligatory'. This puts extra financial pressure on already stretched family budgets. (Chapter 7)

The number receiving free school meals has risen by nearly 40 per cent since 1991. However, the service provided is not uniform. Some LEAs provide a full 'dining centre' meals service, others 'cash cafeteria' services. A few LEAs provide a residuary 'sandwiches only' service for those entitled to free meals. LMS has muddled this wide geographical variation, allowing some schools to reintroduce a meals service after their parent LEA had abandoned it. A residuary meals service is highly stigmatising for children from poor families. Both cash cafeterias and dining centres allow children entitled to free meals to be stigmatised, but with the former the 'free meals' child can usually be more easily identified. What of the situation for those children from poor families just above income support levels? As with other education costs at the point of service delivery, meal costs vary widely between LEAs – from 55p to £1.26 a meal in 1993. If you have children at school, it is better to be poor in Humberside than it is in Kingston-upon-Thames. (Chapter 8)

RESULTS AND OUTCOMES

The clear 'bottom line' for education has to be the results and outcomes from schooling. How have different groups fared? Here we are largely restricted to the easily measurable test, examination results and staying-on rates. There has clearly been a rapid overall increase in qualifications achieved at school, staying-on rates and entry to higher education since the late 1980s. Much of this can be attributed to the introduction of GCSE, and economic and demographic changes, rather than to changes in educational policy. However, the consistent story so far is that the gap between different social groups remains wide. Worse, there is some evidence at the primary level that the apparent decline in reading levels in the late 1980s and early 1990s was most marked in disadvantaged areas. At secondary level, proportions of the age group obtaining 5+ higher grade GCSEs and staying on at school shows a diverging trend, with the most advantaged areas moving further above the poorest between 1988 and 1994. Young people from poorer districts are still much more likely to leave school at the minimum point without qualifications. And there is a growing number of young people aged 16 and 17 who drop out of education, training and work, and receive no benefit. The short and long-term prospects of moving into secure employment and out of poverty must be slim for this group.

Our overall conclusion is of an increasingly fragmented and divided educational service, with a strong shift away from the idea of a unified national education system. In one sense this is in line with the aim of government policy, to create greater diversity of *institutional* provision, with the national curriculum and its assessment providing the common linking threads. But as we have seen, this diversity can too easily be translated into divisions and inequalities in provision. This much more fractured educational system unfortunately reflects the more fragmented wider social and economic structure, where social, economic and spatial factors interact to influence 'life chances'. Overall these educational inequalities are as wide as ever, with some evidence that the gap is growing. It is too early to say authoritatively how far recent educational policies have contributed to this divide; they certainly have not helped to reduce it, and have diverted scarce energy and resources to other sometimes wasteful ends.

Our conclusion is that many children in poor areas continue to receive far less than a first-class education. This view is widely shared. As the HMI study on *Access and Achievement in Urban Education* concluded, 'the rising tide of national educational change is not lifting these boats'.[2]

To point out what is wrong with the present position and policies is perhaps the easy part. To conclude on a more positive note we end with some concrete suggestions for improving education for children from poor areas. First, we should begin to think of ways of removing the 'barriers to learning' in such areas, and second of extending opportunities, creating 'real choices'. There is nothing wrong with 'choice' itself ; rather that 'choice' in an already very unequal world may mean no choice at all for some, and for others the opportunity to 'opt out' and pull up the drawbridge to preserve their advantage.

REMOVING 'BARRIERS TO LEARNING'

'Barriers to learning' probably affect all children to varying degrees but have particular impact on the urban disadvantaged. These are the very factors that reduce opportunity and make choice illusory. 'Barriers to learning' may include lack of finance, lack of health, lack of care – having insufficient money to buy books or clothes for school attendance, missing school because of illness or over-tiredness, or lacking the support of a well-motivated family or home. They can be defined in terms of nutritional levels, as in the example of the Victorians' 'penny dinners'; or, in a current example, in terms of lack of childcare which frustrates families' attempts to enter the job market and so bring more income into the home.

For individual children, these barriers to learning arise from chronic and worsening poverty and result in:

- insufficient money to purchase adequate clothing, or to contribute to the ever increasing list of activities or items for which 'voluntary contributions' are required;
- inadequate nutritional levels in the home, or ill-health, which affect school attendance;

and are exacerbated by living in an LEA which

- allocates to schools a comparatively small proportion of the budget by way of 'social needs';
- is allocated by the government a comparatively small amount under the AEN element in its SSA;
- has little or no pre-school provision;

- offers little or no grant support for post-school provision;

and by attending a school which

- has insufficient funds from the LEA to buy enough textbooks, paper and pencils for its pupils, or to maintain its crumbling buildings
- raises limited funds from external sources because it serves a catchment area where parents cannot afford to contribute;

and may also

- experience an additional barrier of having no or restricted choice as regards school.

These 'barriers to learning'

- affect both parent and child: for example, the absence of pre-school provision means that children lose out on high quality educational provision, while parents cannot get a job because of lack of childcare;
- are stigmatising: for example, schools may organise dinners so that children 'on free school meals' are immediately identifiable, or school trips so that children or parents claiming exemption from payment feel they 'stand out';
- are structural: 'access' and 'choice' depend on where you live;
- result in exclusion from education, or lack of participation.

The key elements in 'barriers to learning' – in a negative sense – are thus to do with *access*, *choice* and *funding*. Choice, through a complex combination of funding arrangements, parental expectation and expertise, and children's performance, tends to reinforce rather than break down social class inequalities. Thus the market analogy is flawed: for some children, 'choice' functions as a *barrier* rather than an *avenue* to learning. The reforms that have taken place are nominally about choice and standards – but actually they have been about institutional change; that is, how the system is structured. They have not been about entitlements, except in curriculum. 'Choice' should be read in the context of 'equity', not the 'market'.[3]

But in a more positive sense, the concept of 'barriers to learning' presupposes rights and entitlements. Children have a right to education. This means equal chances for all of high quality education, free at the point of delivery. This implies that children should be in a fit state to learn and free from restrictions on 'entry' or 'access'. It also implies differential allocations of resources. Further, if children are to arrive at the school gates in a fit state to learn, then certain things follow – for example, an entitlement to pre-school in preparation for school; in short, the right to have one's educational needs met.

EXTENDING OPPORTUNITIES AND REAL CHOICES

In its plea for 'educational priority areas' (EPAs) nearly 30 years ago the Plowden Report called for schools in deprived areas to be given priority. 'The first step must be to raise the schools [in these areas] with low standards to the national average; the second quite deliberately to make them better.'[4] The overwhelming evidence is that we have as yet hardly reached the first step.

In the 1960s there was little robust evidence on the best ways of raising educational levels, or 'what works' in the American jargon. But 30 years on we are far better placed and know from many studies that children from poor families are more affected – for good or ill – by their experiences in school than children from more advantaged homes. We know that the following can have lasting effects for children from poor families:

- high quality pre-school provision;
- special reading schemes such as Reading Recovery;
- reductions in class size for young children;
- more 'effective' schools;
- parental involvement.

If all these were combined together into a comprehensive programme, the educational chances for children from poor families would be dramatically improved.

These measures would begin to tackle the disadvantages imposed by the education system on children from poorer homes. But they cannot in themselves address the wider effects of poverty. The problems that poorer children confront in an educational service which penalises and compounds their parents' poverty form part of a general picture; a comprehensive strategy is needed to overcome child and family poverty. Such a strategy requires an increase in child benefit to a realistic level, a minimum wage set at a level sufficient to prevent poverty wages, and the availability of high quality and affordable childcare provision. These are just some of the measures CPAG believes to be necessary.

This does not reduce the significance of educational reform. To ensure that all children have the education which will, among other things, provide them with the skills necessary to find employment at a decent level of income, is a crucial first step in breaking that vicious circle in which poor children become poor parents with poor children. It cannot be right that having denied large numbers of families an acceptable standard of living we then prevent their children from having the full range of educational experiences and facilities which are on offer for the children of the better off. Action on the education divide is urgent, but will be effective only if it forms part of a broader strategy to end child poverty, both now and in the future.

NOTES

1. Department for Education, *Choice and Diversity: a new framework for schools*, Cm 2021, 1992.
2. Office for Standards in Education, *Access and Achievement in Urban Education*, HMSO, 1993, p45.
3. See G Walford, *Choice and Equity in Education*, Cassell, 1994.
4. Central Advisory Council for Education, *Children and Their Primary Schools*, HMSO, 1967, para 151.

BIBLIOGRAPHY

Adler, M (1993): *An Alternative Approach to Parental Choice.* NCE Briefing No. 13. London: National Commission on Education.

Adler, M, Petch, A and Tweedie, J (1989): *Parental Choice and Educational Policy.* Edinburgh: Edinburgh University Press.

Advisory Centre for Education (1992): *Exclusions.* Bulletin No. 45, January.

Ball, S J, Gewirtz, S and Bowe, R (1992): 'Circuits of schooling: a sociological exploration of parental choice of school in social class contexts'. *British Educational Research Association conference paper,* Stirling.

Berger, N (1990:): *The School Meals Service: from its beginning to the present day.* London: Northcourt House.

Bissett, L and Coussins, J (1982): *Badge of Poverty: a new look at the stigma attached to free school meals.* London: CPAG.

Bone, M (1977): *Preschool Children and the Need for Day Care.* OPCS. London: HMSO.

Bourne, J, Bridges, L and Searle, C (1994): *Outcast England: how schools exclude black children.* London: Institute of Race Relations.

Bradshaw, J and Millar, J (1991): *Lone Parent Families in the UK.* DSS Research Report 6. London: HMSO.

Bridgewood, A and Savage, D (1993): *General Household Survey 1991.* OPCS. London: HMSO.

Bull, D (1980): *What Price 'Free' Education?* London: CPAG.

Bull, D: '"Free" education: shirking and shifting responsibilities'; in Bull, D and Wilding, P (eds 1983): *Thatcherism and the Poor.* London: CPAG.

Bull, D and Glendinning, C: 'Access to "free" education: erosion by statute and stealth', in Bull, D and Wilding, P (eds 1983): *Thatcherism and the Poor.* London: CPAG.

Bullock, A and Thomas, H (1994): **The Impact of Local Management of Schools**. University of Birmingham.

Burghes, L and Stagles, R (1983): *No Choice at 16: a study of educational maintenance allowances.* London: CPAG.

Campbell, R J and Neill, S R (1993): *Four Years On: the failure of curriculum reform at Key Stage 1.* University of Warwick, November 1993.

Central Advisory Council for Education (1967): *Children and Their Primary Schools.* London, HMSO.

Centre for Policy Studies (1988): 'Advice to the Secretary of State'. In Haviland, J (ed): *Take Care Mr Baker!* London: Fourth Estate.

Chartered Institute of Public Finance Accountants (1994): *Education*

Statistics 1992-93, Actuals, CIPFA, October 1994.

Chubb, M and Moe, T (1990): *Politics, Markets and America's Schools.* Washington, DC: Brookings Institution.

Cohen, B (1988): *Caring for Children: services and policies for childcare and equal opportunities in the United Kingdom. Report for the European Commission's Childcare Network*. London: Commission of the European Communities.

Cohen, B and Fraser, F (1991): *Childcare in a Modern Welfare System: towards a new national policy*. London: Institute for Public Policy Research.

Coleman, J S (1969): 'Equality of educational opportunity' in *Harvard Educational Review*, Special Issue: *Equal Educational Opportunity*. Cambridge, Mass: Harvard University Press.

Commission of the European Communities (1990): *Childcare in Europe 1985-1990.* CEC.

Community and Youth Workers Union (1992): *Youth Work and Community Work into the 21st Century: policy statement.* Birmingham: CYWU.

Cox, C B and Boyson, R (eds 1975): *The Fight for Education:* Black Paper 1975. London: Dent.

CPAG (1985): *Burying Beveridge: a detailed response to the Green Paper: Reform of Social Security*. London: CPAG.

Davie, R, Butler, N R and Goldstein, H (1972): *From Birth to Seven: a report of the National Child Development Study (NCDS)*. London: Longman.

Department for Education (1992): *Choice and Diversity: a new framework for schools*. Cm 2021. London: HMSO.

Department for Education (1992): *Statistical Bulletin 14/92*, July 1992. London: DFE.

Department for Education (1993): *Statistical Bulletin 22/93*, student awards in England and Wales. London: DFE.

Department for Education (1993): *Statistical Bulletin, 26/93*, women in post-compulsory education. London: DFE.

Department for Education (1994): *Pupils with Problems*, Circular 10/94: exclusions from school. London: DFE.

Department for Education (1994): *Statistical Bulletin 4/94*, education expenditure from 1979-80. London: DFE.

Department for Education (1994): *Statistical Bulletin 6/94*. June 1994. London: DFE.

Department for Education (1994): *Statistical Bulletin 11/94*. London: DFE.

Department for Education (1994): *Statistical Bulletin 13/94*. London: DFE.

Department of Education and Science (1972): *Education: a framework for expansion*. London: HMSO.

Department of Education and Science (1973): *Nursery Education*. Circular 2/73.

Department of Education and Science (1975): *Nutrition in Schools*. London: DES.

Department of Education and Science (1984): *The Education Welfare Service: an HMI enquiry in eight LEAs.* London: HMSO.
Department of Education and Science (1985): *Education for All: the report of a committee of inquiry into the education of children from ethnic minority groups.* Cmnd 9453. Swann Committee. London: HMSO.
Department of Education and Science (1986): *City Technology Colleges: a new choice of school.* London: HMSO.
Department of Education and Science (1986): *School Attendance and Education Welfare Services.* Circular 2/86. London: DES.
Department of Education and Science (1988): *The Education Reform Act: local management of schools.* Circular 7/88. London: DES.
Department of Education and Science (1989): *Discipline in Schools. The Elton Report.* London: HMSO.
Department of Education and Science (1991): *UK Statistics of Education,* 1991 edition.
Department of Social Security (1993): *Households Below Average Income: a statistical analysis 1979-1990/91.* London: HMSO.
Department of Social Security (1994): *Annual Statistical Enquiry.* London: Government Statistical Service.
Department of Social Security (1994): *Households Below Average Income, 1979-1991/92.* London: HMSO.
Douglas, J W B (1964): *The Home and the School.* London: McGibbon and Kee.
Douglas, J W B, Ross, J M and Simpson, H R (1968): *All Our Future: a longitudinal study of secondary education.* London: Peter Davies.
Douse, M (1985): 'The background of assisted place scheme students'. *Educational Studies,* 11(3), 211-17.
Education Committee of the House of Commons (1994): *A Common Funding Formula for Grant Maintained Schools.* London: HMSO.
Education Committee of the House of Commons (1994): *The Disparity in Funding Between Primary and Secondary Schools.* London: HMSO.
Edwards, T, Fitz, J and Whitty, G (1989): *The State and Private Education: an evaluation of the Assisted Places Scheme.* Lewes: Falmer Press.
Eggleston, J, Dunn, D and Anjali, M (1986): *Education for Some: the educational and vocational experiences of 15-18 year old members of ethnic minority groups.* Trentham Books.
Emmerich, M and Lewis, J (1991): *Unemployment in Oxfordshire.* Oxford: Oxfordshire County Council.
Essen, J and Wedge, P (1982): *Continuities in Childhood Deprivation.* Aldershot: Gower.
Fitz, J, Power, S and Halpin, D (1993): 'Opting for grant maintained status: a study of policy making in education'. *Policy Studies,* 14(1), 4-20.
Fletcher-Campbell, F, Keys, W and Kendall, L (1994): *Discretionary Award Provision in England and Wales.* Calouste Gulbenkian Foundation.

Floud, J E, Halsey, A H and Martin, F M (1956): *Social Class and Educational Opportunity*. London: Heinemann.

Fourth Report of the Select Committee (1993): *The DFE's Expenditure Plans 1993-4 to 1995-6*. London: HMSO.

Friedman, M (1965): *Capitalism and Freedom*. Chicago: University of Chicago Press.

Glendinning, C with Dixon, P: 'School meals: privatisation, stigma and local "autonomy" in Bull, D and Wilding, P (eds 1983): *Thatcherism and the Poor*. London: CPAG.

Glennester, H and Low, W (1990): 'Education and the welfare state: does it add up?' In Hills, J (ed): *The State of Welfare*. Oxford: Oxford University Press.

Goodman, A and Webb, S (1994): *For Richer, For Poorer: the changing distribution of income in the United Kingdom, 1961-91*. London: Institute for Fiscal Studies.

Gorman, T and Fernandez, C (1992): *Reading in Recession*. Windsor: NFER.

Gray, J, Jesson, D and Tranmer, M (1993): *Boosting Post-16 Participation in Full-Time Education: a study of some key factors. England and Wales Youth Cohort Study. ED Research Series Youth Cohort Report No. 20*. London: Department of Employment.

Green, A (1994): *The Geography of Poverty and Wealth*. Warwick: Institute of Employment Research.

Halpin, D, Power, S and Fitz, J (1991): 'Grant-maintained schools: making a difference without being different'. *British Journal of Educational Studies*, 39(4), 409-24.

Halsey, A H and Floud, J E (1957): 'Intelligence tests, social class and selection for secondary schools'. *British Journal of Sociology*, 3(3).

Halsey, A H, Heath, A and Ridge, J M (1980): *Origins and Destinations*. Oxford: Oxford University Press.

Her Majesty's Inspectorate (1990): *Responsive Youth Work: the Youth Service and urgent social needs*. London: HMSO.

Her Majesty's Inspectorate (1993): *Effective Youth Work in Clubs and Projects*. London: HMSO.

Hillgate Group (1986): *Whose Schools? A radical manifesto*. London: Claridge Press.

Hirsch, D (1994): *School: a matter of choice*. Paris: Centre for Educational Research and Development, Organisation for Economic Co-operation and Development.

Howes, C (1990): 'Can the age of entry into child care and the quality of child care predict adjustment in the kindergarten?' *Developmental Psychology*, 26(2), 292-303.

Imich, A (1994): 'Exclusions from school: current trends and issues'. *Educational Research*, 36(1).

Independent Schools Information Service (ISIS) (1994): *Annual Census 1994.*

Istance, D, Rees, G and Williamson, H (1994): *Young People Not in Education, Training or Employment in South Glamorgan.* Cardiff: South Glamorgan Training and Enterprise Council.

Jesson, D, Gray, J and Sime, N (1991): *Participation, Progress and Performance in Post-Compulsory Education. England and Wales Youth Cohort Study. Research and Development No. 64, Youth Cohort Series No. 15.* Sheffield: Sheffield University Division of Education.

Joshi, H (1991): 'Sex and motherhood as handicaps in the labour market'. In Maclean, M and Groves, D (eds): *Women's Issues in Social Policy.* London: Routledge.

Joshi, H (1992): 'The cost of caring'. In Glendinning, C and Millar, J (eds): *Women and Poverty in Britain in the 1990s.* London: Harvester Wheatsheaf.

Karabel, J and Halsey, A H (1977): *Power and Ideology in Education.* New York: Oxford University Press.

Kozol, J (1991): *Savage Inequalities: children in America's schools.* New York: Harper Perennial.

Kumar, V (1993): *Poverty and Inequality in the UK.* London: National Children's Bureau.

Lake, M (1991): 'Surveying all the factors'. *Language and Learning,* June.

Lazar, I and Darlington, R (1982): *Lasting Effects of Early Education: a report from the Consortium for Longitudinal Studies.* Monographs of the Society for Research in Child Development, No. 195, vol. 47, Nos. 2-3. Chicago: University of Chicago Press.

Lee, T (1990): *Carving Out Cash for Schools: LMS and the new ERA of education.* Centre for the Analysis of Social Policy, University of Bath.

Lee, T (1992): *Additional Education Needs and LMS: methods and money 1991-2.* Centre for the Analysis of Social Policy, University of Bath.

Local Schools Information (1994): *Guide to the Issue of Opting Out.* London: LSI.

Lowndes, G A N (1969): *The Silent Social Revolution: an account of the expansion of public education in England and Wales 1895-1965.* London: OUP.

Maclagan, I (1993): *Four Years' Severe Hardship: young people and the benefits gap.* London: Youthaid/COYPSS/Barnardos.

Macmillan, K (1977): *Education Welfare: strategy and structure.* London: Longman.

Martin, J and Roberts, C (1984): *Women and Employment: a lifetime perspective. The report of the 1980 DE/OPCS Women and Employment Survey.* London: HMSO.

McCallum, I (1993): *'Testing seven year olds – performance and context'. Projecting school rolls and assessing performance.* London: London Research Centre.

McLean, A (1987): 'After the belt: school processes in low-exclusion schools'. *School Organisation,* 7(3), 303-10.

Melhuish, E and Moss, P (1991): *Day Care for Young Children: international perspectives.* London: Routledge.

Meltzer, H (1994): *Day Care Services for Children: a survey carried out on behalf of the Department of Health in 1990.* OPCS. London: HMSO.
Ministry of Health (1968): *Day Care Facilities for Children Under Five.* Circular 37/68.
Modood, T (1993): 'The number of ethnic minority students in British higher education: some grounds for optimism'. *Oxford Review of Education,* 19(2), 167-82.
Moore, D (1990): 'Voice and choice in Chicago. In Clune, W and Witte, J (eds): *Choice and Control in American Education,* vol. 2. London: Falmer Press.
Morris, M and Griggs, S (1988): *Education – the wasted years? 1973-1986.* Lewes: Falmer.
Mortimore, J and Blackstone, T (1982): *Disadvantage and Education.* Aldershot: Gower.
Mortimore, P, Sammons, P and Stoll, L (1983): *School Matters: the junior years.* Wells: Open Books.
Moss, P (1994): 'Statistics on early childhood services: placing Britain in an international context'. In Ball, C: *Start Right: the importance of early learning.* London: Royal Society for the Encouragement of Arts, Manufacture and Commerce.
National Association of Head Teachers (1993): *Resources in Education 1993-4.* London: NAHT.
National Audit Office (1991): *Repair and Maintenance of School Buildings.* London: HMSO.
National Commission on Education (1993): *Learning to Succeed: a radical look at education today and a strategy for the future.* London: Heinemann.
National Confederation of Parent Teacher Associations (1991): *The State of Schools in England and Wales.* London: NCPTA.
National Union of Teachers (1992): *NUT Survey on Pupils' Exclusions: information from LEAs.* London: NUT.
National Union of Teachers and University of Leeds (1993): *Testing and Assessing 6 and 7 year olds: the evaluation of the 1992 Key Stage 1 National Curriculum assessment.* London: NUT.
New York State Department of Education (1991): *New Compact for Learning.* Albany, NY: New York State Department of Education.
Noble, M, Smith, G et al (1994): *Changing Patterns of Income and Wealth in Oxford and Oldham.* Oxford: Department of Applied Social Studies and Social Research, University of Oxford.
Office for Standards in Education (1993): *Access and Achievement in Urban Education.* London: HMSO.
Office for Standards in Education (1993): *Education for Disaffected Pupils.* London: OFSTED.
Office of Population Censuses and Surveys (1986): *General Household Survey 1986.* London: HMSO.
Organisation for Economic Co-operation and Development/Centre

for Educational Research and Innovation (1993): *Education at a Glance: OECD indicators.* OECD: Paris.

Osborn, A F and Butler, N (1985): *Ethnic Minority Children: a comparative study from birth to five years.* London: CRE.

Osborn, A F and Milbank, J E (1987): *The Effects of Early Education.* Oxford: Clarendon Press.

Osborn, A F, Butler, N R and Morris, A C (1984): *The Social Life of Britain's Five Year Olds. A report of the Child Health and Education Study.* London: Routledge and Kegan Paul.

Owen C and Moss, P (1989): 'Patterns of preschool provision in English local authorities'. *Journal of Educational Policy*, 4(4), 309-28.

Penn, H and Riley, K A (1992): *Managing Services for the Under Fives.* Harlow: Longman.

Plowden Committee (1967): *Children and Their Primary Schools: a report of the Central Advisory Council for Education.* London: HMSO.

Postlethwaite, N (1988): *Science Achievement in Seventeen Countries.* Oxford: Pergamon Press.

Prais, S (1986): 'Educating for productivity: comparisons of Japanese and English schooling and vocational preparation'. *Compare*, 16, 121-47.

Prais, S and Wagner, K (1985): 'Schooling standards in England and Germany: some summary comparisons bearing on economic performance'. *NIESR Economic Review*, 112, 53-76.

Pring, R (1987): 'Privatisation of education'. *Journal of Educational Policy*, 2(4), 289-99.

Ralphs Report (1973): *The Role of Training of Education Welfare Officers.* London: HMSO.

Roberts, K and Chadwick, C (1991): *Transitions into the Labour Market: the new routes of the 1980s. A study of transitions 1984-87. Research and Development No. 65, Youth Cohort Series No. 16.* Sheffield: Sheffield University Division of Education.

Rogers, W S and Roche, J (1991): *The Children Act 1989: a guide for the Education Service.* Milton Keynes: Open University.

Rutter, M and Madge, N (1976): *Cycles of Disadvantage: a review of research.* London: Heinemann.

Sallis, J (1994): *Free For All? a brief history of state education including summaries of all recent legislation.* London: CASE.

Sammons, P (1995): 'Gender, ethnic and socio-economic differences in attainment and progress: a longitudinal analysis of student achievement over nine years'. *British Educational Research Journal*, 21(4).

Schweinhart, L J, Barnes, H V and Weikart, D P (1993): *Significant Benefits: the High/Scope Perry Preschool Study through age 27.* Monographs of the High/Scope Educational Foundation No. 10. Ypsilanti, Michigan: High/Scope Press.

Scottish Education Department (1992): *Placing Requests in Education*

Authority Schools. Statistical Bulletin Edn/B6/1992/13. Edinburgh: Scottish Education Department.

Seebohm Report (1968): *Report of the Committee on Local Authority and Allied Personal Social Services.* Cmnd 3703. London: HMSO.

Silver, H and Silver, P (1991): *An Educational War on Poverty: American and British Policy Making 1960-1980.* Cambrige: Cambridge University Press.

Sime, N, Pattie, C and Gray, J (1990): *What Now? The transition from school to the labour market amongst 16 to 19 year olds. England and Wales Youth Cohort Study. Research and Development No. 62, Youth Cohort Series No. 14.* Sheffield: Sheffield University Division of Education.

Simon, B (1991): *Education and the Social Order: 1940-1990.* London: Lawrence and Wishart.

Smith, D J and Tomlinson, S (1989): *The School Effect: a study of multi-racial comprehensives.* London: Policy Studies Institute.

Smith, G (ed 1975): *Educational Priority: Vol. 4: the West Riding Project.* London: HMSO.

Smith, T (1992): 'Family centres, children in need and the Children Act 1989'. In Gibbons, J (ed): *The Children Act 1989 and Family Support: principles into practice.* London: HMSO.

Social Science Research Unit (1994): *Health in Primary Schools.* London: Institute of Education.

Sumner, R and Hutchinson, D (1990): *Resources in Primary Schools.* Windsor: NFER.

Sylva, K (1994): 'The impact of early learning on children's later development'. In Ball, C: *Start Right: the importance of early learning.* London: Royal Society for the encouragement of Arts, Manufacture and Commerce.

Tizard, B and Hughes, M (1984): *Young Children Learning: talking and thinking at home and at school.* London: Fontana Paperbacks.

Tizard, B, Blatchford, P, Burke, J, Farquhar, C and Plewlis, I (1988): *Young Children at School in the Inner City.* London: Lawrence Erlbaum Associates.

Townsend, P and Davidson, N (eds) (1982): *Inequalities in Health.* Harmondsworth: Penguin.

Utting, D, Bright, J and Henricson, C (1993): *Crime and the Family: improving child-rearing and preventing delinquency.* London: Family Policy Studies Centre/NACRO/Crime Concern.

van der Eyken, W (1984): *Day Nurseries in Action: a national study of local authority day nurseries in England, 1975-1983. Final Report December 1984.* Bristol: Department of Child Health, University of Bristol. Mimeo.

Walford, G (1988): 'The Scottish Assisted Places Scheme: a comparative study of the origins, nature and practice of the Assisted Places Scheme in Scotland, England and Wales'. *Journal of Educational Policy,* 3(2), 137-54.

Walford, G (1994): *Choice and Equity in Education.* London: Cassell.

Wardhaugh, J (1990): 'Regulating truancy: the role of the education welfare service'. *Sociological Review*, 38, 735-64.

Wardhaugh, J (1991): 'Absent without leave: state responses to school non-attendance'. *International Studies in Sociology of Education*, 1, 209-23.

Whitty, G, Edwards, T and Gewirtz, S (1993): *Specialisation and Choice in Urban Education: the City Technology College experiment.* London: Routledge.

Wilkinson, R G (1994): **Unfair Shares**. Barkingside: Barnardos.

Willms, J D and Echols, F (1992): 'Alert and inert clients: the Scottish experience of parental choice of schools'. *Economics of Education Review*, 11(4), 339-50.

Wilson, H and Herbert, G W (1978): *Parents and Children in the Inner City*. London: Routledge and Kegan Paul.

Witherspoon, S and Prior, G (1991): 'Working mothers: free to choose?' In Jowell, R, Brook, L and Taylor, S (eds): *British Social Attitudes: the 8th report.* Aldershot: Dartmouth/SCPR.